Silver-- The People's Metal

Ryan Jordan

Email: rjordanster@gmail.com

Web: ryanpjordan.com

"The truth is incontrovertible. Panic may resent it, ignorance may deride it, malice may distort it, but, in the end, there it is."

Winston Churchill

Table of Contents

Prologue by David Morgan

When I first began writing about silver nearly 15 years ago, not many investors cared about the white metal-- one of the worst performing assets around at the time. Even fewer recognized the need for honest money, for money that cannot be debased or devalued by banks and governments. In the late 90s, everyone was buying the hottest internet stock, and central banks were still dumping gold, a metal widely viewed as useless for modern, civilized people. Many believed in the fantasy that we lived in a "new era" where tangible assets were unnecessary.

Well, that was then and this is now. A lot can change in fifteen years when it comes to people's perceptions about money and investing.

After several Wall Street scandals, after two stock market implosions, and the collapse of the residential real estate market-- or any number of other mishaps over the past decade and a half-- some people are giving the precious metals another look.

Another change since 1997 has been the growing chorus of voices online who have taken up the cause of getting the word out about investing in monetary metals, especially silver.

Some people are rediscovering an old tried and true fact: silver is the people's money. What I mean by this is that central banks and others who think they run the world still own a lot of gold, but no silver. You can argue how much has been swapped, loaned out, or held by more than one institution, but the central banks still own the gold. They have access to it. On the silver side, however, the white metal has been dismissed by the banking system. This is the case even as silver has been money for thousands of years--it is a monetary metal. But people's understanding of silver's monetary aspects are coming back. You can see this with new online depositories for helping people own the metal (like silver123.net, goldmoney.com or bullionvault.com), and you can see this in all sorts of new efforts to allow the precious metals to circulate right along with central bank paper money. In Mexico, you have Hugo Salinas Price's effort to bring back the silver libertad coin, for example. In the United States, there have been many state efforts to allow for consumers and businesses to use silver and gold in everyday transactions. Utah, for one, recently passed a law allowing for people to purchase goods and services with silver. We are getting to the point where as people's frustrations boil over concerning indebtedness, lack of job security, taxation, or inflation, they will seek value based money. This will cripple the ability of the banking establishment to keep the price low, or to otherwise discourage people from saving in real money. Of course the banking system should not be surprised at this development: after stiffing savers with zero percent interest rates, is it any wonder that savers are redefining what money is?

One of the more outspoken proponents of alternative currency systems is Representative Ron Paul. Whether or not you support all of Ron Paul's policies, you should respect the man for warning early on about the dangers of reckless speculation in the banking sector and irresponsible spending in the public sector. Representative Paul never believed that we were living in a new era, he never went along with the idea that debt does not matter, or that there is never going to be a time to pay the piper, as it were, when debts come due.

Recently an online video made the rounds on youtube concerning Representative Paul's questioning of Federal

Reserve Chairman Ben Bernanke during his testimony on the economy. Representative Paul held up a silver coin to Federal Reserve Chairman Ben Bernanke during the question period, and asked the Chairman to recognize the value of alternative currencies. To paraphrase, Dr. Paul pointed out how the silver ounce he was holding will actually buy MORE gas today than in 2006. "That is preservation of value," asserted Dr. Paul. "The market has spoken regarding silver's value as money." Paul went on to remind Bernanke how "money comes into effect in a natural way, not by an edict, not by governments declaring what should be and should not be money." Finally, Dr. Paul asked Bernanke, "Why is it that we can't consider this option: you (Bernanke) love paper money; I love constitutional money. Why don't we allow these currencies (silver and paper money) to run parallel? " Dr. Bernanke refused to answer the question, saying simply he would be happy to talk to Ron Paul about the issue privately. I would like to listen to that conversation.

Whether or not some bankers care much about bringing back gold and silver as currency, individual people are already voting with their feet in terms of trying other means of preserving the purchasing power of their hard-earned savings. I already mentioned how savers are getting nothing on supposedly safe bank deposits. You are not going to get any interest on it. But some savers have done quite well buying gold and silver these last 15 years. And the same fundamental reasons that have led to the appreciation of precious metals over the last 15 years are still very much in place. Some would actually say there are even stronger. So my advice is simple: Save in real money.

But above and beyond simply trying to grow your wealth, there is a more important principle at work behind the increased interest in silver. No matter how much money you accumulate in the physical silver markets, or in derivatives markets, no matter how much money each person makes in life overall, it pales to the most important thing, and that is freedom. If you have accumulated great wealth, but don't have the freedom to spend it where you wish, or say what you wish-- in other words if you have lost your freedom in the process of making individual wealth- I think you've given up way too much. It is the freedom of ideas, the freedom of the press, things that have slowly eroded over time by the powers that be that we need to defend. For me the movement to bring back silver is part of this larger movement, part of a larger awakening of people asserting their rights.

I hope you realize that there is nothing more important than being a free people. In terms of spreading this idea, I believe the internet is key. The internet really is the epitome of the free market of ideas. On the internet, everyone who has access to a computer can learn about health, about education, or music, or nearly any other topic. The internet is broad-based. It is also up to you to take advantage of it, to read and think and do your own due diligence. I was taught early on not to believe everything you read, hear, or even see. You need to learn to think for yourself. There is a great deal of truth on the internet, though, particularly about the corruption pervasive throughout the global political and economic structure.

Getting at the truth isn't easy; neither is it easy to get people to realize that everything is not as it appears to be. To try to influence younger people in particular, I like to make online videos because I believe in the power of spoken and visual communication. Almost two years ago, I did a video that was a take-off on the film "The Matrix" and the famous scene when Morpheus gives Neo the red pill, which enables

Neo to truly understand the nature of his oppression. In my video a silver coin was given instead of a red pill. The idea was to remember what silver stands for. It is not just an asset, it is not just a way to make money. Buying silver is about making a statement, it is about dissenting from a society where you are taught only to be a consumer, where you are made to judge your worth as a human being by your ownership of material things. I made the video because I wanted young people to get the idea that in today's society, for the most part, people are born a debt slave, they live a debt slave, and they die a debt slave. It may be hard for many to avoid this reality, but, as has been said, a journey of a thousand miles begins with a single step.

I encourage you to do something—anything-- that resonates with you to stand apart from the prevailing herd mentality on money or on life in general. Especially for younger people who are looking at difficult job prospects, who are dealing with student indebtedness, who are facing an uncertain future. It is time to put away the wasteful behaviors of an earlier era; to stop living your life by the dictates of conventional society, if at all possible. The time has come to seek out off-beat ways to face head on the possibility that the consumer-driven, debt based prosperity of the past may not be there for you in the future. This does not mean the end of the world; it does mean that you have to be prepared.

I think the book that Ryan has written sums up well not only the reasons why you might be able to make some money with silver, but—more importantly—why the silver story represents the kind of awakening described above. The book makes a good argument for being realistic, for being honest, and for trying to live a life that is consistent with principles. One of the slogans I use for my website and videos is: "buy real, get real, be real." I think the story laid out in the pages that follow is a good reminder for anyone who claims to love freedom, and to honor dissent, that the time has come to really start putting your money where your mouth is.

As always, wishing you health above wealth and wisdom beyond knowledge,

David Morgan
Youtube: silverguru
Twitter: silverguru22
Web: www.TheMorganReport.com
Email: silverguru22@hotmail.com

Preface: Why I Wrote a Book About Silver

Has it ever dawned on you that the way you think about a certain issue, topic, or event could not be more different than the majority of people around you? Have you ever been made to feel as though you were crazy for feeling a certain way about the world? Well, this is sort of how I first felt when I began explaining to people the reasons why I was buying gold and silver several years ago. Of course today (mid-2012) fewer people see buying silver as crazy after the events of the past four or five years. Still, I know that too few people take gold or silver investing seriously. I think this is a mistake. A rather large mistake, actually.

For reasons that even I can't entirely explain, two years ago I began to write about why investing in gold and silver was not, in fact, a dangerous, risky, or bizarre thing to do. I had some spare time on my hands (having recently been downsized myself as a college instructor—another thing that only encouraged my already cautious view of the future) and decided to act on this strange sense of purpose to do my part and help set the record straight regarding an asset that too few owned. I also wanted to defend the worldview of those of us who buy these metals.

People sometimes liken owning gold or silver to a religion. To this accusation I plead guilty. But I contend that the religion of gold and silver is growing. The gold or silverbug religion preaches skepticism towards authority, reminds people how they cannot have something for nothing, and openly challenges many of the downright fraudulent aspects of our current financial and political system. This religion has many silent and not so silent followers out there.

7

It may not mean that everyone is rushing out to convert every asset they have into metal, but I sense that more and more people are coming to understand why skepticism (some might even say pessimism) has not been bred out of the human gene pool. In other words, being willing to accept and deal with the truth-- no matter how painful or hard to confront—isn't such a bad idea after all. In this current world, I would call it smart and prudent, if not highly profitable.

If you read the following book as a speculator, or as someone who is looking for places to put "hot money," you should understand that people like me, who invest meaningful percentages of their savings in gold and silver, are not going away. In fact, our numbers are growing. As a protest against banks who treat savers like garbage with zero percent interest rates, I would not underestimate what I call the moral imperative of owning the precious metals, an imperative not arising from a need to make a fortune, but out of a desire to stand up for certain ideals. I believe the little statements, the little actions you take can have an effect and can produce results in others that are sometimes surprising. We often underestimate how important small actions are in terms of changing the habits and mindsets of others. Our behavior can make people think about their relationship to a debt-based financial system which leaves a lot to be desired.

In the final analysis, then, this book is about more than just silver. It is about all of the ways that people can prepare to live in what has been euphemistically called "the new normal." Unfortunately, I do not believe we have seen the end of the financial and political turmoil of the past decade. This is not meant to scare anyone, and it does not mean that the end of the world is at hand. It is just the way it is.

It has been said that the Chinese used to curse people by telling them, "may you live in interesting times." We certainly live in interesting times, but I am not so sure that we are cursed. The challenges we face can, if confronted properly, provide for the growth of character at least for individuals, if not for nations.

I hope you accept the challenge made in this book to think about your world in unconventional ways, and to acknowledge that even as our lives are often dominated by impersonal technologies, bureaucracies, corporations, or governments, that the power of the individual is one that cannot and should not be underestimated.

Introduction
Silver: The Investment of Our Age

Although this book is more than about getting rich quickly, I do think you could (emphasis on *could*) make a lot of money in silver—even as I don't think that is the only reason to own the white metal. You also need to remember that some people not only make a lot of money—they spend it too. So don't necessarily expect this market to bail you out if you are not cautious or careful with the management of whatever wealth has been entrusted to you.

But having got those caveats out of the way, here would be my sales pitch if I were trying to convince you that silver could, in fact, be the most lucrative investment you could make:

What if I told you about an investment that could be the next Microsoft, the next Apple, ready to make a return of possibly hundreds (if not thousands) of percent? Would you think that I was some sort of scam artist or con-man? Maybe nuts? You might just dismiss me with the old saying, "if something sounds too good to be true, it probably is." I have to admit, as someone who prides himself on being realistic about a lot of things, I share your skepticism about any investment sold as a can't-lose proposition. I understand where you are coming from, especially if you have watched a stock portfolio or a real estate investment turn south over the past decade. Maybe you think that the best you can do is be happy with boring, sub-par returns on bonds or bank deposits, or some other "safe" investment. Maybe you have given up on the challenge of growing your nest egg for the future. Maybe you have stopped trying to take risk in order to make your money work for you because of prior bad advice.

Well, in the pages that follow, I want to make a respectable, intelligent appeal for you to own silver. I want you to consider how the social mood, or the spirit of this age, where people have been scarred by financial crises, and where there are looming fears about inflation, means that silver can move a lot higher. In a world of rediscovered concerns about resource scarcity, "peak" everything, and in a world where many wonder how hundreds of millions of people can join the middle classes in the emerging world without higher commodity prices, the silver price could continue to move in one direction: up. Silver might just make a move fit for the record books. I want you to understand the odds of this happening, and take action. I don't want you to say to me or anyone else that no one ever told you about the silver story.

I believe silver is the investment for our age, meaning that the white metal's price benefits more than other investments from the changing practices and beliefs in our modern economy and society. To take one example, in terms of investing, the years since 2007 have represented the nail in the coffin for the idea that your home was a personal ATM machine, always available for you to fund whatever your heart desired because the price of one's home always increased. To add insult to injury, the collapse of real estate values occurred less than ten years after the destruction of another, related idea: that your 401(K), made up mostly of stocks, would only increase year after year (preferably at an annual rate of 15%), and that inconvenient things like savings and actually providing for your own future out of your present income were irrelevant.

In short, the idea that historical reality did not apply to people who lived between roughly 1982 and 2007 has, I believe, been discarded. This is true whether or not everyone wants to admit it, or whether or not everyone wants to acknowledge the dramatic shift which is occurring beneath their feet. A shift towards caution and perhaps toward realism is quickly enveloping the broader society around us. As I mentioned above, if you have savings, in this new environment you need to learn to position yourself correctly for what lies ahead. There is a war going on, a war being fought by central bankers to stave off the bogeyman "deflation" (which really just means deflating bank assets and other related investments). Savers have been sacrificed in this battle against deflation, and are now being paid nothing. Central bankers, in a perverse way, want people to shift into real assets, but they have to be careful, because in the extreme their policies can lead to a point where no one wants paper currencies at all. You have to understand that we live in a world where there is a heightened risk of sustained, very high inflation for things we need for survival, even as other assets (like homes or stocks) stagnate, or even move lower. We live in a brave new world now, a world quite unlike the boom years of the 80s and 90s. This change needs to be met head-on by anyone trying to realistically manage their savings.

To historians, this shift is not surprising, though, since history is characterized by cycles, by people or institutions swaying from one extreme to the other. For every action, there is a reaction, for every bubble there is a crash. There are moments when people's perceptions snap out of a rut, and move in an entirely new and unexpected direction. Whether you are aware of it or not, you, me, everyone is riding the waves of history.

Investing in silver is more than just about taking a gamble on a white piece of metal. The turn toward silver has everything to do with morality, politics, social conventions, and about simple survival through tough times few saw coming. So allow me to introduce you to all of the things a rising silver price is saying about our world and the people who think they lead it, and why the silver story—a story about a relatively obscure investment becoming more and more popular—is far from over.

The Silver Story

The silver story is about sizing up the craps table called modern capitalism, and understanding that someone is always the patsy or the mark- someone is always on the losing end in the zero sum game of markets and money. The silver story is about the existence of cartels, insiders, and people who distort or manipulate prices. The silver story is about the arrogance of central planning. It is about self-reliance. The silver story is about dissent, candor, frankness, freedom of speech, freedom of thought, a defiant independence against the state or the corporate controlled media. The silver story is about the blogosphere, about alternative media making a stealth attack on official accounts of reality from those dispensing propaganda. The silver story is about hidden knowledge, about those who suspect that average people are always in the dark about who is really in charge, about who is really pulling the strings. A story about escaping the matrix of debt, about standing apart from the herd, apart from group think, from Orwellian mind-control schemes, the silver story is about ponzinomics, about system apparatchiks masquerading as experts who act like they know what they are doing. The silver story concerns the limits of the American Dream- a dream that maybe you can only believe if you are asleep (so said George Carlin).

The silver story is about the epitome of wastefulness, of a mistaken belief in abundance. The mistaken belief that new technologies can always be relied upon to drill deeper, or to extract more and more miniscule amounts of ore, so as to satisfy society's need for abundant, cheap amounts of a metal which can then be tossed away. Rather than conserve or preserve silver, governments and individuals consumed silver over the course of the twentieth century—billions of ounces of it in tiny amounts that can never be recovered. Now, silver is a metal that is truly rare, whereas not that long ago it was practically in the same category as base metals like copper, lead, or zinc. The silver story, then, is also about scarce resources in a world that seems to pretend scarcity is impossible.

The silver story is about finding the courage to be honest about the lies around you. The lie that debt and wasteful spending can go on forever. The lie that you "own" a home when you practically have to mortgage your first born to pay for it. The lie that it is somehow patriotic to consume. The lie that we have free markets. The lie that government programs are always going to be there for you.

It may be that some of us who have decided to invest in the white metal have a pessimistic, foreboding side- or it may just be that we are the only ones truly awake. After all, conventional society cannot stand to hear the truth that the cycles of boom and bust, of the birth, maturation, and decline of financial and political systems apply to all people. No one can avoid them. No matter how hard leaders try to maintain the confidence game- and scheme with efforts to paint the tape of group thought patterns- something turns, a tectonic shift occurs, and the world slips out of the hands of those who thought they called the shots. This is the troubling history of economies, societies, governments, and political systems. This is also the case with investments or forms of saving—and it is the case with silver.

For years and years, large banks and paper players (along with governments) were able to convince everyone from average people to wealthy investors to part with their physical silver. This is because a lot of silver is simply traded or held on paper—a pretty important issue that needs to be understood by anyone investing in this metal. Excessive selling of paper silver (along with governments dumping real stockpiles) helped to dupe many investors into further releasing their silver onto the market. All of this dumping allowed for silver users to get access to silver at levels lower than the cost of production, because above-ground stockpiles filled the gap from a lack of mine supply and recycled silver. This is called a "silver deficit" and it existed for nearly 20 years. The fact that silver was selling for less than its cost of production (what it costs to take it out of the ground) was part of the reason why Warren Buffett bought so much of it in the late 1990s (even as he sold out a few years later).

But nothing stays the same, and eventually, other people picked up on the fact that something was terribly wrong not just with the silver market, but with many other aspects of our financial and political world. Many people no longer see the world the way they once did. There are many examples of a shifting popular consciousness, ranging from the Tea Party in the United States, to anti-Wall Street demonstrations, to uprisings in the Middle East, or other mass movements. As the world adjusts to some sort of new economic "normal," everything is questioned, people move to think in different ways. The distrust, anger and disappointment expressed in these movements represent several reasons for the price of silver to move higher.

What Makes Silver So Special?

Silver, a monetary metal (chemical symbol Ag, atomic number 47) has the greatest thermal and electrical conductivity of any metal known to man. Silver is arguably the most reflective element in the periodic table. Silver's durability and malleability ranks very high among the earth's elements, and so do its antibacterial qualities. Silver possesses an excellent musical resonance (part of the reason people want silver bells and not aluminum bells.) With the advent of photography, silver halide revolutionized how people took and preserved images, and silver oxide is still needed if you want an actual, real photograph. Silver (with copper) is among the oldest and most widely used monetary metals in history, and has a long history in commemorative artifacts and jewelry. In the English language, a word for eating utensils is silverware, a testament to the metal's use in cutlery.[1]

To the Incans of Peru, silver came from the moon: "tears of the moon," as they put it. Along with gold-- which they said was the "sweat of the sun"—Incans mined silver as a way to worship the deity. Across time and space, spanning cultures and the rise and fall of empires, silver (along with gold) has often been thought of as a "precious metal," an important linguistic and cultural statement regarding the white metal's value for humans. As with the Incans, many cultures have used silver in their religious artifacts or idols. Throughout Western history, silver has been at the center of the world economy, the driver of empires, and an asset that has probably cost just as much if not more blood and treasure to extract than gold. Today, as the world faces sobering realities ranging from debt crises to concerns about resource growth, silver is once again slowly coming onto people's radar screens, and for good reason.

Silver has been money in more places and has been used by more people than has gold throughout history, even as silver is rarer today than at almost any other time in history (especially relative to gold). With the advent of the industrial revolution, silver became a go-to metal for everything from cameras, to dishwashers, indoor plumbing, television sets, computers, cell phones, adhesives, and now solar technology (in addition to others uses.) The industrial applications for silver far exceed gold, which ironically is part of the reason why silver is so undervalued and rare: government and banks dumped all the silver they could dump so as to satisfy industrial demand which gave markets the impression of limitless supply for the white metal. As you will read below, this mistake has led many to wonder whether or not a true industrial shortage in silver is possible in the coming years. As will also be written below, this market "mistake" has been encouraged by all sorts of pushers of "paper" silver, leading many to cry foul and to call the silver market one of the most manipulated markets in modern times.[2]

The value of all of the silver for investment is only 60-70 billion dollars more or less; all of the silver jewelry and other artifacts are maybe another 500 billion dollars. Compared to the world's gold, possibly valued at 8 trillion dollars, it would not take many gold investors to try to diversify their assets into silver for the white metal's price to jump. And this leaves out any new investors into silver, or any increase in industrial demand. The same is true, as will be explained below, regarding silver futures and other paper representations of the metal. If those who simply "play" silver in the futures markets decided to buy and store the real metal, once again the silver price would explode without any new investors entering the market. These facts should tell you something both about the miniscule nature of the silver market, as well as how silver could be poised for a moonshot in terms of price. I can't make any guarantees, but by the same token you have got to understand your odds with any "investment" (which is usually nothing more than a speculation), and your odds with silver are about as good as they come.[3]

Silver is a metal few people own, but everyone needs. As silver analyst David Morgan often says, you could take all of the gold out of the world and hardly anyone in industry would care. But if you took all of the silver out of the world, there would be a major problem for anyone who wanted computers, cell phones, medical equipment, or solar panels. Silver is an extremely important, valuable metal. And yet much of this silver actually gets destroyed. Currently, it is just not economical to try to save this silver. But if the silver price were to rise, and more people were to hoard it as an investment, more silver would be conserved. So in addition to needing silver as an investment hedge, you may actually be doing the economy a favor by saving silver![4]

For many, however, the real reason to own silver will be to distance oneself from currency debasement and asset price deflation brought about by consumer downsizing in the years ahead. Things change, and sometimes they change quickly or in ways that are difficult for most people to perceive. And this brings me to another fact that is incredibly bullish for silver: the world of the 1990s- the world where silver holders couldn't dump their metal fast enough- might as well be 100 years ago in terms of what has transformed our economy and our world over the last ten years. Yes, you might look around and see that you own a similar house, or drive down a similar street, or perhaps go to a similar job (if you are still employed) as ten or fifteen years ago, but this familiarity really only masks tectonic shifts in the treatment of savers, and in the future of a credit-based, consumption-based, American-led economic world.

And however similar you may think your life still is to the life you lived ten or fifteen years ago, there is another difference worth noting: enough people around the world are redefining the role of tangible assets as vehicles for savings. After 2008, many ordinary people realized that they might just be on their own. For many, rampant corruption and insider cronyism typifies the political and regulatory landscape, most infamously with events like the Madoff scandal, subprime fraud, the MF Global heist, or the bailouts in general. Many asked, where was their bailout? The joke was on the retail investor, it seemed- these little people were not a part of the in-crowd that could make money by their associations with Wall Street or Washington.

So try as they might, the humpty-dumpty of investor confidence in all-things leveraged can't be put back together again by salespeople or politicians, or anyone else trying to push the same old, same old investment philosophy. The time has come for investments that fit the mass mood of a more cautious, conservative, skeptical, and (at least in some cases) angry investing public.

I am part of this public, maybe you are as well. I buy silver not because I believe in doom and gloom; I buy silver because I believe in reality. And reality has been a long time coming for many people who believed things that not only weren't true, but were hazardous to their financial well-being.

Keeping An Open Mind: The Only Way to Succeed in the
World of Saving and Investing

I think part of the silver story has to do with keeping an open-mind. I want to make an important appeal to you, the reader, to do just that regarding what you are about to encounter below. If you are someone trying to save for your future, whether it be for a house, for education, or for retirement, you need to learn a very important lesson, one that I also try to impart to my students: learn to think outside the box, and learn to question whatever you "think" you know about the world of saving, speculating, or investing.

Maybe you think that a bank account, or a portfolio of stocks, or a bond, or residential real estate is the best way to preserve or grow your hard-earned savings. I will agree that each of these savings vehicles have a strength: bank deposits are insured by the government, stocks can give you a chance to profit from fast-growing industries, bonds can pay interest, and real estate is something everyone needs. But all four of the above investment (yes, even real estate) are not REAL assets. What do I mean? I mean that all four of these investments are either paper investments, or they need more and more people to go into debt, to spend, to consume in order for them to become more valuable (or some combination of the above.)

As a tangible asset that is paid for in cash (little borrowing is usually involved, at least among retail investors), silver- along with other tangibles like gold, gemstones, or truly rare collectibles- does not need more debt or more consumption to move higher. And if you hold it in physical form, silver certainly is not a paper asset.

You may have also heard something about "silverbugs" or "goldbugs" and that they are a little off, or all live in a bunker or something along those lines. You may be thinking to yourself: silver is something you would only buy if you agree with people who are waiting for the end of the world. Let me explain to you why this is the wrong attitude to have.

First of all, the silver story has something for everyone, optimist or pessimist. Since the metal could potentially see very high demand from industry, if you believe there will continue to be strong demand for consumer electronics, or solar energy, or cell phones, or cleaner medical devices, silver will accelerate in price in the event of a sustained industrial uptick in demand. In other words, silver does benefit from economic growth. Moreover, this acceleration will be far greater than other metals, whose supplies are larger or more elastic (meaning their supplies can more easily respond to demand.)

Silver could explode higher both because stockpiles are so low, but also because silver has a dual role, or as I like to say, silver has more than one jet engine strapped to it. Silver is a tangible investment you make to guard against the ravages of inflation. So any industrial user trying to get their hands on the metal is always competing against those of us who also see silver as real money or as an inflation hedge. With a market as small as silver, this kind of competition could lead to a dramatic price explosion. It could even lead to a company like DuPont or some other silver user deciding that it is willing to pay any price for the white metal, thus driving the price up several TIMES in short order. Please note that this did in fact happen to the palladium market in the late 1990s, and palladium does not have the kind of monetary demand that silver does.[5]

Signs That You Might be a "Silverbug Extremist"

But let me get back to the issue of silverbug extremists, or the end of the world types who are so often associated with both monetary metals.

Maybe you think that you have nothing in common with the hard money advocates who hoard silver coins in their gun safe or in their floorboards, or in PVC pipe in an "undisclosed location." Well, after the events of the past few years, I bet that you have far more in common with the "silverbug extremists" than you in fact realize. Are you upset with bank bailouts? Are you concerned about the effects of zero percent interest rates on savers, or on the elderly? Do you find a lot missing in terms of the honesty or integrity of mainstream media reports, say, about something like inflation? What about conventional politicians- are you all that happy with who they are or what they stand for? Do you go to the grocery store and see packages shrinking or prices rising? Are you struggling with surging costs for college tuition, higher costs for health care, or wonder about the sustainability of something like Social Security?

If you answered yes to any or all of the above questions, I am sorry to inform you that you are already well on your way to becoming a "silverbug extremist."

You may not live in a bunker in Montana, you may not consider yourself a survivalist, you may look down on the scores of conspiracy theories peddled by many on the fringe of the internet, but if you are concerned about the destructive power of the state, of the corrosive power of corporatism, or are not happy at all regarding the behavior

22

of our "leaders," or that they really are "leaders" in any sense of the word, then you might just be a "silverbug extremist."

I for one, do not live in a rural compound surrounded by barbed wires and lasers. In fact, not only am I a conventional middle class person from a family of Orange County, CA realtors, but I even attended Princeton University where I wanted to be a history professor. Pretty mainstream, even "establishment" by some standards. But I was always taught to value honesty and integrity, unfortunately two things that I don't see a lot of in our current financial system (or other institutions for that matter).

At the end of the day, I chose to put most of my (small) amount of money into gold, silver, and (some) mining stocks because I was livid after the crisis of 2008, a moment representing the culmination of many stupid policies pushed around for years. I was fed up; I also felt that the Federal Reserve's zero percent interest rate policy was insane, that it was (and is) risking a disorderly currency collapse for the dollar, and that this policy means that savers are irrelevant to our current financial system. It feels as though we are slipping toward a totalitarian future, like that described by George Orwell or Aldous Huxley. Buying gold and silver for me is one small, defiant gesture against the rottenness around me. I didn't buy them to make a fortune, I bought them because I felt there was no place left to go.

Buying gold and silver is about *peaceful* civil disobedience and protest. Their purchase is done in the spirit of encouraging more realistic thinking about what our system can and cannot offer people, more realistic thinking toward a more sustainable economic future both monetarily and in terms of material resources. I also feel that people have to be mentally prepared for the unexpected, or for things that seem to come out of the blue (yes, like economic misfortune or political turmoil). This is because history teaches that no one, really, is immune from all of the bad things that Americans have grown accustomed to believe can never happen to them.

But to get back to my larger point, at the end of the day there are many, many reasons for silver to launch to the moon. My political or personal beliefs or fears are just that: beliefs and fears. They are not really relevant for gold and silver in many ways. You should keep this in mind whenever you want to simply dismiss gold and silver as "doomsday" investments. This is simply not the point.

Higher Silver Prices Don't Necessarily Mean Systemic Collapse

No, the reality is that 1 trillion dollars going into the silver market is simply one trillion dollars going into the silver market. Since there are tens and hundreds of trillions of dollars or wealth or credit in our global financial system, one trillion dollars moving into the silver market does not in my mind necessarily represent a currency collapse—at least if it happened slowly, over time. But it would move the silver price to north of 500 dollars, or over 15 TIMES higher than where it is right now (around 30 dollars). One trillion dollars going into silver only means that a lot of capital is trying to find a home; abused capital yes, but not necessarily capital that is fleeing the burning building of a "collapsed" global financial system. (Understand that if we actually saw 20 or 30 percent of the world's capital try to go into silver, we would be talking about 10,000 dollar *silver*--- perspective counts, and keep this in mind when you think that a silver price rising from say, 40 to 100 dollars represents the "end of the world.")

There is a cycle to everything, every investment out there comes in and out of vogue, in and out of fashion. All you have to do is look at a chart of the silver price and see that it has steadily been moving up for nearly a decade now. To many market observers, this is spectacularly bullish. This chart pattern is also telling you a lot more about mass psychology than any talking head on T.V.

If you don't have genuine tangible assets as part of your savings, you are simply missing out on a chance to grow your savings. You aren't only making a political statement, or doing something negative or pessimistic. No, what you are really doing is being open-minded about how to diversify your assets. When you buy silver, you also understand that just because the nice person in the broker/dealer office, or the person who manages your 401(k) says something to be true, well, you need to remember that they are only human. They make mistakes, they are not God. The same is true for all of the central planners or central bankers who told us nothing was wrong with the economy in the years before 2007. These individuals, in many cases, have nearly exhausted the confidence and goodwill of the investing public. In many ways, they do not deserve your money.

In the end—and this is important--you need to have the power and the courage to think for yourself. No one else will do this for you; any great success in the world of investing or finance derives from the courage to stand on your own.

Chapter 1
The Big Picture: Crisis Investing

2008: The Last Straw

If you are reading this book, you shouldn't need much introduction to the financial crisis of 2008 (a crisis that to many people has not ended). For me, watching people talk about liquidity crises, or how the banking sector was in danger of going under from bad loans, or seeing late night meetings where central bankers attempted to bailout companies only to see stocks head lower the next day, reminded me a lot of 1929. You have to bear in mind that I have a Ph.D in U.S. history and that I teach at the college and university level. So you could say that I spend a lot of time living in the past. For me, October 2008 looked a lot like 1929, all the more so because at the time I was teaching an introductory history class on the 20th century, and we happened to be covering the issues and events surrounding the 1929 crisis during that fateful October a few years back. The similarities were striking, and it only confirmed in me and my students that, as has been said of money and markets, "the game does not change, and neither does human nature." Delusions, illusions, hopes, and dreams from manias vanish with amazing alacrity, replaced by a sobering new world. To go back to the 1930s, it took a while before contemporaries realized what the market crash of 1929 had actually meant. It was only in the fullness of time that people would use that year, 1929, as a demarcation point between two radically different worldviews, distinguishing a world of careless optimism from one of stark realism.

As with the crash of 1929, the crash of 2008 came from an unsustainable way of life (if it can be called that), based on borrowing, and borrowing, spending, and then some more borrowing. For my entire life, this had been the way people in my hometown, my home region, and my home country lived financially. I guess you could also call it keeping up with the Jones'- and there was this amazing notion that it could go on forever. You know, rules that normally apply to individuals-- rules like if you don't pay your bills on time, you go bankrupt-- didn't quite seem to apply to this world. There was always some new game in town, always some new way to make a quick buck. Whether we are talking about real estate booms, the junk bond boom, the tech boom, or the boom in consumer borrowing, I had lived a good portion of my life watching and wondering about the bizarre world around me, wondering if what I was seeing was in fact real. I also saw the careless attitude toward indebtedness spread around the world, whether we are talking about European debt-binges, or housing speculation in China. It looked as though many aspects of the Orange County, CA life had gone global. I guess it is true that everything starts in California. (If this is true, you may want to watch out in the years ahead.)

I was pretty familiar with the devil-may-care attitude in residential real estate. Real Estate, for better or for worse, has been a major employer in Southern California, as it has been throughout many parts of the United States. Like it or not, real estate was an industry which employed (and still employs) millions of people. The Housing Sector really became a huge component of economic "growth" in the years from roughly 2002 to the market crash of 2008. Residential housing epitomized the confidence game of American "capitalism" in the opening years of the 21st century.

Unfortunately, the boom produced by housing was artificial, and it is likely not coming back anytime soon.

As with everything else in life, many average people involved in real estate are often just along for the ride. A lot of times, they did not care to think about why so much attention, interest, and money was thrown at housing, an asset that inflated because of more and more lending that seemed to be able to go on forever. But the California real estate market is a symbol of the kind of hubris that grows out of optimism and confidence. Unfortunately, what goes up, comes down, and this applies not only to the housing sector, but most of the American economy and financial system.

Cognitive Dissonance and California Real Estate

Many members of my family, at some point or other, were either real estate agents, or landlords or involved in the escrow industry, or some combination of the three. This was not unusual for Southern Californians in the last century or more. California was "sold" to Midwestern and Eastern Americans from at least the 1880s (when railroads came through) as the dream land that could cure all of the ills of the more boring (and cold) life back east. Real estate promoters played an important role in selling the California dream to others in the U.S. and around the world. You could say that southern California was built on hype- it epitomized the shameless promotion, the sky-is-the-limit mentality so characteristic of American "capitalism." It may be my conceit, but California in so many ways is a microcosm of all that is good and all that is lacking in the American economic model.

Don't get me wrong, I'm not necessarily knocking the wide-eyed optimism of Americans. One of the greatest

28

character traits of Americans is their ability to believe that every fantasy can come true- the kind of can-do individualism that many around the world have come to envy. This was the optimism that crossed the Appalachians, built canals, constructed cities and railroads, that irrigated deserts like those in Utah in California, and that later contributed to the automobile, the computer, or the Internet. There were also plenty of natural resources such as minerals and oil in the West that were tapped and used to fuel the idea (some would call it illusion) that there were/are no limits to growth. But remember- sometimes your best quality is also your worst attribute.

This discovery has led to what psychologists will call cognitive dissonance, namely, where you can't make sense of how such a seemingly wonderful world can in fact be, in some way, fraudulent or deceitful. How can the optimism, happiness, positivity of my home region lead to such potential unhappiness, disappointment, or failure? This is something maybe you struggle with too. This is part of the process of awakening, part of the process of learning to live with reality as part of the silver story, instead of running away from it, instead of mocking the people who politely, skeptically remind you to look over your shoulder.

Borrow Till You Drop

It is worth looking back at how every American from the individual to the government has been able to believe that reality does not apply to them. Or more accurately, the effort of trying to repeal the laws of history which clearly showed that going into too much debt never really has a happy ending. The desire to pretend that history does not count, has influenced many modern-day Americans, and it eventually led to the banks, in league with the government, convincing more and more people to go into debt for this "American Dream" of residential real estate ownership.

If we look at the experience of the 1920s and 1930s, the American government essentially doubled-down on the roulette wheel of credit and indebtedness. The crash in stocks and real estate during the last Depression (which pulled both markets down 75-90%) represented the ugly side of the increasing expansion of credit in the modern United States. The 1920s had been the first time many Americans could buy household items with installment plans in conjunction with newer mortgage options, and the decade also saw the explosion of stock margin accounts, where average people could all of a sudden buy equities with nearly no down payment. We all know how badly that ended.

But the resulting crash after the Roaring 20s did not stop the need for central planners to keep the wheel of credit rolling. The New Deal extended mortgage financing to more homeowners on ever more generous terms. Many organizations, such as the Home Owners Loan Corporation, and the Federal Housing Administration (which still exists) were created to dramatically lower down payment requirements. These organizations also enabled a vast increase in home refinancing. Remember, before the 1930s, you generally had to put anywhere from 50% to 100% down to buy a home. It was only after the 1930s and 1940s that more and more Americans were allowed to put progressively smaller amounts of money into homes that they were "buying." In truth, most Americans were taking part in a ponzi scheme, hoping that more and more people would go further and further into debt to finance this dream that your home could be your personal ATM machine. It took a while, but a whole new generation of Americans are coming to realize that if it sounds too good to be true, it is, and so it was with the idea that your home was the best "investment" you could make.[1]

Another Big Lie: the national credit card can never be maxed out

Another reason for the "keeping up with the Jones'", borrow, borrow, borrow till you drop mentality, has been due to the United States having a very useful national credit card with foreigners. It is called a "reserve currency." It basically means that for whatever reason, foreigners want to hold dollars. Why might that be you ask?

In order to explain the reason for the power of the U.S. dollar we have to go back to World War II. Keep in mind that before the war, Europe (and especially London) had previously been the financial capital of the world. But by 1945, with the European continent in shambles, many countries bankrupt, and with the British Pound taxed out by both wars and a huge empire, another country was taking the place of Britain as the main financial center of the world. This country was the United States. The United States emerged from World War II virtually unscathed, and for quite some time was already the strongest industrial power in the world. The U.S. possessed plenty of natural resources. America had more gold than anyone else, and she possessed more than half the world's oil (yes you read that correctly), and tons of other things like coal or natural gas. The U.S. also boasted a powerful industrial base that was leading the way with new technologies like the car, the television, or the computer. The average American in 1950 made more than 15 times a comparable European. The U.S. was the place to invest, and it was little wonder that many would say the dollar "was as good as gold." When you couple this with the military might, all the thousands of nuclear warheads and fleets of naval ships, you understand why the rest of the world would want to use the U.S. dollar as a store of wealth and as a means of transacting trade.

And so we had, after 1945, the U.S. Dollar Reserve system. The United States was able to force other nations to use its currency if those countries wanted to trade with the U.S, or be protected by the American military. Oil is priced in dollars, as is gold. The establishment of the petrodollar occurred in the 1970s during the height of the Cold War, and further encouraged Americans to confidently believe that cheap natural resources were their birthright. But there are unfortunate consequences of these developments. A dangerous legacy of the dollar reserve system is that more dollars are held outside the country than within the country. This bears repeating: foreigners are the ones holding most of the dollars these days. Might this change? Why are we so certain that central banks around the world will continue to hold 60% of their currency reserves (savings, basically) in dollars? Can you imagine what might happen if foreigners found out that the main engine for economic growth- namely consumer indebtedness- was not going to be there? What might happen if other nations acted on the fact that the average American is tapped out, and can't be the central figure in this debt based, consumption game? If there is a perception that the US can't grow out of its monumental debt, there is a problem. If countries (like, say, Iran or China) decide to barter for goods instead of using the dollar (which has been reported as of early 2012), this is not good news for dollar holders. (Jim Sinclair of jsmineset.com has done some excellent reporting on Asian and other developing nations beginning to shun the dollar, by the way.)

Might there be concern that the United States is not the country it once was? This is of course where discussion of the future of the U.S. dollar as a reserve currency also turns into a referendum on national pride. Many Americans don't like people telling them that their country isn't as all-powerful as it once was. They don't like hearing that empires decline, and that they often decline because of their own decadence and corruption. But facts are what they are: and many economics and scholars (if not publicly then privately) wonder how much longer it is going to be before foreigners begin to reduce further their holdings of dollars and dollar-denominated bonds in a disorderly fashion (it is already happening, but slowly). Mind you, I am not talking about a complete collapse of the dollar, necessarily. Simply a diversification by other people away from the dollar. When this happens, the value of the dollar declines, and the value of real things goes up. Pretty simple, supply and demand. Still, I am always surprised by how many American savers or retirees have not prepared accordingly for this very likely outcome, based on historic fact. It already has begun, but the effects have not been completely felt, and the decline has been gradual. So far.[2]

The Zombie Banks

The reckless attitude spawned by the national credit card of a reserve currency certainly applied to American banks. You know, those miraculous institutions that no matter what any economist may tell you, do create money out of thin air (the phrase is: "lend money into existence.") On one level then, banks are a Ponzi scheme, but on another level fractional reserve banking allowed for all sorts of average people to get loans to build things, invent things, or consume things. Banking can be likened to atomic energy, in that it can be amazingly powerful in both profoundly good and bad ways. Yet many times, people forget how banking, while alluring and powerful, is also incredibly dangerous.

The evolution of installment plans, credit cards, derivatives- all of these things sprang from the modern banking idea that you really can have it all. In our modern world, take it or leave it, for better or for worse, a large part of the lifestyle we have is because of the incredible increase in the amount of this money, or this debt. But as with everything else in life: YOU CANNOT HAVE YOUR CAKE AND EAT IT TOO. Unless, of course, you are a banker. This is because in our modern world, bankers know that tails they win, and heads they win. Why? Simple: the bankers know the government has their back, at least for now. And this certainly was the case during the bailout of 2008. One of the more egregious examples of this, of course, came from AIG, who had made numerous bad bets with "derivatives" and got itself bailed out at the expense not so much of the US taxpayer, as the global dollar holder (remember, more dollars are held outside the country than within it, but foreigners will only tolerate so much abuse...)

As of this writing, American central bankers are saying what one sea captain once said during the Civil War: "damn the torpedoes; full speed ahead!" In other words, American bankers don't care very much about lessening the value of our currency. This is pretty much the view of Ben Bernanke, who is the current head of the Federal Reserve. The one lesson he believed he took away from the last Great Depression was that the Federal Reserve and other central banks did not do enough to bail out the banking system, to make sure that this legalized Ponzi scheme was propped up at all costs. He wanted to make sure that large banks would not fail completely. Other establishment economists and central planners, for example Larry Summers, who also helped to allow banks to take on nightmarish amounts of leverage with the repeal of the Glass-Steagall Act, have similarly stated something to the effect that the solution to this crisis of confidence in spending is in fact to double down with even more spending and debt (and bailouts). In other words, you have to use debt to solve a crisis caused by debt (if that doesn't sound insane, you should stop reading this book.)

These men find it perfectly normal that impaired bank balance sheets were made alright by what has been termed "mark to make believe" accounting. By April of 2009, FASB rule 157 was suspended, and this meant that all of the bad real estate loans made to people with little or no income, and that included little to no down payment, can be valued at whatever price the banks find necessary in order to make their balance sheets look good for investors. Once they have accomplished this, they can entice more investors back into banking stocks. A great idea, no?[3]

Fallacies in the Fed, Central Planning, Fiat Currencies and Debt

And more than simply being a problem with the Americans, the model of lying about the dangers of debt so as to get more people to go into it, has infected a large part of the western world. Many around the world also believe that indebtedness can go on forever without there ever being a time to pay the piper.

One of the over quoted examples of establishment thinking that debt does not matter and does not necessarily have to pose much of a threat to people came from the mouth of Federal Reserve Chairman Ben Bernanke. In the event of "deflation," meaning bank assets and other speculative investments losing value, men like Bernanke maintain that "a determined government can always generate higher spending and hence positive inflation."[4] I translate this speech to mean that the central bankers will do whatever it takes to flood the system with liquidity and that central planners are always ready and able to both spend and devalue their currencies enough to somehow avoid serious losses to asset values of the major banks.

The problem with Bernanke's argument is that, in fact, central bankers have always claimed that they know how to smooth out the business cycle--- and they have always failed. Moreover central planners and their allies among the economics profession have also spent considerable time trying to explain how entities like the Federal Reserve, if simply given one more chance, really will demonstrate that they are in control of the global economy. History, of course, provides sober reminders that this over-confidence is flat wrong. If we look back at the last Depression, we see many examples of the Federal Reserve and other central banks failing in their mandate to generate price stability and strong employment. Between 1928 and 1933, pretty much across the world, stock markets, real estate values and farm prices declined over 75% and global GDP fell by something close to 25%. The severity of the Depression came as a shock to some because it occurred less than twenty years after the creation of the Federal Reserve, an institution supposedly dedicated to stopping these types of severe economic contractions.

Moreover, this second major banking crisis of the twentieth proved difficult for the central planners to shake, even as they tried hard to do so. In the early 1930s, foreign central banks lent significant sums to insolvent entities: for example, the Bank of England sent money to Austria in 1931 after the failure of its version of Lehman Brothers, called the Creditanstalt. In addition, many foreign central banks- again led by England- later turned to currency devaluation as a solution to the Depression (I hope this sounds familiar). Beginning in September 1931, Great Britain went off the gold standard, followed quickly by Japan, Scandinavian countries, and, in early 1932, by Germany. Most famously, the British Pound fell about 35% in less than one year, but the Depression still proved difficult to shake. The point of all this is to remind people to be very skeptical of any central banker trying to tell you to trust him that he is in charge of the economy and that policy makers have now figured out some new tool to avoid or otherwise smooth out the business cycle.[5]

Some will say that Roosevelt's reform agenda (such as closing banks or establishing the SEC) restored confidence in the banking system, but I would respond that such reform only occurred after the stock market lost nearly 90% of its value. So for me, I have to wonder if, like someone suffering from a hangover, the market had puked up everything it was going to before Roosevelt began his reforms. The intangible thing called confidence may have been ready to come back on its own, with or without government intervention. Either way, the nation had to endure incredible pain before reforms were put into place, reforms which also, in the long term, helped to set up the very private/public partnership that could be used to further the dependence of Americans on credit. People were encouraged to go back to believing that credit expansion has no consequences and that Depressions can in fact be regulated or legislated away.

I want to be clear that I am not trying to claim that criminals should not be held accountable for their financial crimes, or that attempts to create a safer, less levered financial system are all bad. What I am trying to say is that business depressions- when people or banks refuse to borrow and spend to keep other people employed- can be likened to a force of nature. Policy elites will claim that all you need to keep the economy afloat is to make sure that banks are stocked with funds. Others will claim that confidence can be restored by reforms ranging from breaking up banks, or putting the country on a state-sanctioned gold standard, or some other confidence booster, but can the state really mandate or control confidence? How do you encourage banks to lend? How do you ensure that people will want to borrow? If people don't want to borrow, but the banks have been recapitalized, what is stopping banks from pouring money into tangible assets, thus sending prices for needed items like food through the roof at the same time that people are suffering from unemployment or stagnant wages? Put another way, if the real economy wants to contract, but those at the top are getting plenty of money from central bankers through bailouts, this will eventually lead to serious inflation (too much money chasing too few goods.)

Inflation is a policy goal of central bankers using fiat currencies. You need to understand this first and foremost. The issue is whether or not this policy goal can create economic growth or job creation. These policies may simply force people into tangible assets and out of paper forms of wealth.

Inflation is always a threat to savers, but at some times it is a bigger threat than at other times. Regardless, if you are the government, the last thing you would want to do is loudly broadcast or advertise the true nature of inflation. After all, inflation is a hidden tax, and the authorities have become all the more astute in the last couple of decades at hiding this form of taxation from the people. At some point in the 1990s, the U.S. government decided to change how it measured price inflation. You need to understand that this likely was done to save the government from having to make huge increases in the cost of living to retirees on Social Security, since the long term viability of that program has long been questioned (you should know the story by now: too many baby boomers retiring and living longer, mixed with not enough young workers to foot the bill.)

One of the more astute critics of U.S. government inflation measures is John Williams, of shadowstats.com. Williams reminds people that Alan Greenspan (the FED chairman before Bernanke) encouraged the government to stop using the same kinds of goods when putting together a basket of prices. For example, according to Greenspan, if the price of a good steak was going up, people would simply buy hamburger meat, and so the government could claim that hamburger meat was the same as steak, and therefore that the price of beef was not increasing.

I am not making this up.

Moreover, Greenspan began to popularize the idea of "core inflation" which ever so conveniently strips out food or energy prices when calculating inflation. It is almost Orwellian because most of the conventional media outlets will report this "core" inflation as the true measure of price increases or decreases. Of course, doing this had a powerful impact on people's perceptions regarding the purchasing power of their dollar: they were lulled to sleep to ignore that inflation was far higher than what the system was telling them.

This is especially true because inflation- like interest- compounds. According to Williams, the average rate of inflation by using the older CPI numbers has really been much closer to 7 or 8% for the last 30 years!! The older CPI number (which Williams calls the SGS Alternate CPI) means that 1 dollar in 1980 is now worth only 12-15 cents. His inflation data also means that the price of gold should be roughly 5000 dollars an ounce (based on the average 1980 price of 600 dollars). Contrast this with the newer CPI: a 1980 dollar will have only declined to about 40 cents, give or take, and the price of gold should be about 1750 dollars an ounce. The compounded difference between the old and new CPI, in terms of the dollar equals an additional 50% loss of purchasing power of a dollar over 30 years.[6]

You should probably also realize that the "gross domestic product" would be revealed to be negative, if you properly accounted for the dramatic loss of purchasing power of a dollar contained in Williams' numbers. People innately understand this, I think. They know that it now takes two incomes for middle class households just to make what one income made 40 years ago (in many cases, it is less.) But you won't see this on the evening news.

The zero percent interest rate policy, when coupled with government lies about the true nature of inflation, means that wealth is being destroyed at a faster rate than usual. Another way of saying this is that we currently have extremely negative real interest rates. If the true rate of inflation is running at 8 percent, but you are getting effectively zero on your bank deposit, over time you will suffer compounding losses. Remember that an 8 percent loss of purchasing power over 3 years is not simply a loss of 24%-- it is actually closer to a 33% loss of purchasing power.

The above should be common sense: why would the government want to tell you the truth regarding what it is doing to its currency? Why would the government want to advertise that the economy is in a slow-motion decline? The inflation tax is the oldest trick in the book for governments to secretly confiscate the wealth of savers. As I write this, governments and central banks are not only trying to secretly confiscate wealth, but they are doing it at a time of severe economic stress around the world, at a time when many wonder if the global economic confidence game is broken for many years to come.

There have been many people throughout history who have recognized the threat from inflation, by the way, and I think it is important to list several quotes from those in the past who understood the fraud that is government or central bank-sponsored inflation:

"Paper should never be money but only employed as a representative sign of value existing in metals or produce....When the [Chinese] government borrowed the invention from private individuals, and wished to make a real money of paper, the original contrivance was perverted." Ma Twan-lin, Chinese historian, circa 1350

"[Debasement of the currency] is taken into account by few persons and only the most perspicacious. For it undermines states, not by a single attack all at once, but gradually and in a certain covert manner." Nicholas Copernicus, "Treatise on Debasement," 1517

"The reason why [a coin's silver content] should not be changed is this: because the public authority is guarantee for the performance of all legal contracts. But men are absolved from the performance of their legal contracts, if the quantity of silver under settled and legal denominations be altered ... the landlord here and creditor are each defrauded of twenty percent of what they contracted for and is their due." John Locke, 1695

"If the American people ever allow private banks to control the issue of their currency, first by inflation, then by deflation, the banks and corporations that grow up around them will deprive the people of their property until their children will wake up homeless on the continent their fathers conquered." Thomas Jefferson, 1783

"The way to crush the bourgeoisie is to grind them between the millstones of taxation and inflation." V.I Lenin, 1919

"Lenin was certainly right. There is no subtler, no surer means of overturning the existing basis of society than to debauch the currency." John Maynard Keynes, "Inflation and Deflation," 1919

"The first panacea for a mismanaged nation is inflation of the currency; the second is war." Ernest Hemingway (unknown citation)

"Gold still represents the ultimate form of payment in the world. Fiat money in extremis is accepted by nobody. Gold is always accepted." Alan Greenspan, 1966

"No nation in history has ever survived fiat money, money that did not have precious metal backing." Ronald Reagan, 1980

"...Freely floating exchange rates are inherently unstable; moreover, the instability is cumulative so that the eventual breakdown of a freely floating exchange rate system is virtually assured." George Soros, "The Alchemy of Finance," 1987

"High interest rates, withdrawal of subsidies [to the developing world] and floating the exchange rate have further worsened the economy and resulted in instability. Those who benefitted were the currency speculators. Indeed, economic terrorists do not differ from other terrorists." Mahathir Mohamad, Malaysian Prime Minister, September 20, 2002[7]

All of the above quotes should show you how many different people, from different walks of life and political orientations have understood the damaging power of inflation on the savings of ordinary people. Gold and silver know no political party, they have no ideological agenda. You may think that only certain kinds of people are crazy enough to want to own something like silver bullion. I want to explain to you why this is wrong. Any person who is concerned about the future of their savings owes it to themselves to understand why you need precious metals. It really is just that simple. Don't let anyone try to convince you that there is something weird, or dangerous about these metals. They simply represent an important—and arguably first—line of defense against central planners trying to debase the value of other people's money.

There is one last quote regarding precious metals that I wanted to share. I bet you will not be able to guess who was its author:

"Money...serves as a universal measure of value. And only by virtue of this function does gold, the equivalent commodity par excellence, become money."[8]

The author was Karl Marx, one of the founders of modern-day Communism. What does it mean that our current financial system is to the left of Karl Marx? I'll leave that for you to decide.

Chapter 2
Why People Buy Silver (or other precious metals)

It seems every day, more and more people are questioning aspects of this economic system. They are becoming more cautious. They are looking for more conservative places to put their money. Some perhaps regret the dangerous amounts of leverage they took on in the past, particularly in housing, and they have noticed that many of the world's stock markets have gone nowhere (or worse) over the last 10-15 years.

Some people are also regretting how they ignored the monetary insurance provided by metals like silver. Over the last few years, investors have had to relearn sobering lessons from the past. The reasons people throughout history have turned to precious metals are many, and these reasons are just as true today as they were centuries ago.

Silver and gold are easily divisible and standard in composition, nearly indestructible, and they are not generally seen as a necessity of life (such as oil or grains), so there are fewer qualms regarding hoarding them. Gold in particular is especially portable- a million dollars fits in a relatively small box. For silver, its about 60,000 dollars- still not bad. For these reasons, if you are a central banker or someone managing billions (now trillions) of dollars and you want something that is outside the banking system, that cannot be devalued by fiat, that is easy to physically take delivery of and is indestructible, you would turn to precious metals- not bulky and perishable items such as oil barrels or farmland.

Silver and gold are also far more inelastic than other commodities, meaning that when a bunch of demand comes into these markets, you cannot just go out and mine more gold or silver. New mine supply for gold has actually been flat over the past decade or so. There are fewer ounces of gold than there are people on earth- and many fewer above-ground ounces of silver coins, even if there are many more ounces of silver jewelry and other objects like silverware. For all of these reasons and others, precious metals form their own asset class, similar to, but different from other commodities because of their scarcity and their history as money.

Gold and Silver as Money- And What is Money, Anyway?

At this point it is worth reviewing why gold and silver became money in the first place (including in the U.S. Constitution, by the way). It is also important to recall why people have scrambled to get silver and gold during times of instability—something that has occurred repeatedly throughout the past.

For many centuries- and still today in many less developed parts of the world- people have bartered or traded for goods. A pretty simple idea: I trade my bushel of wheat for your cow, or some corn for your cloth. But barter isn't perfect. If I don't want to trade my property for whatever you offer to sell, then there is no trade. Multiply this by thousands of people and trade slows down. This can be a major problem. If I can't get the type of goods I need to keep my farm going or to feed my family, then society as a whole can break down. This is where money comes in. Money is something that many thousands or millions of people agree upon as having value in lieu of exchanging real goods. Throughout history, many things have been money- whether shells or copper, or (today) paper money or credit cards. But gold and silver- indestructible, rare, and easily divisible with a standard composition- have often emerged from failed paper currency experiments as the last assets standing. For most of the last 4,000 years it is safe to say that silver and gold were the most important monetary metals. I maintain that they still are.

However, as you should be aware, there is only so much gold and silver to go around. Yet lots of people want money to do all sorts of things- like building roads, developing farms or businesses, or all sorts of other productive activities that, at least in theory, will benefit the broader society. So overtime the idea of credit evolved with the help of what are called "fractional reserve banks." A fractional reserve bank is a bank that for every ounce of gold, or money, that it has on its books it lends out 1,2, or 40 times as many loans to people in order to enable them to go about their business.

Historian Niall Ferguson claims the first European fractional reserve bank appeared in 1657 in Sweden, called the Stockholms Banco. This bank began the practice of lending in amounts greater than what it possessed as a reserve in precious metal. For example, for every one ounce of gold in its vaults, the bank might lend out the paper equivalent of nine ounces to other individuals, who in turn could put that "money" into another bank, which would further lend out even more money.[1] If you are thinking that this resembles a Ponzi scheme, you would be correct, except that this scheme is legal and is backed by state power. To be fair, this Ponzi scheme has created great wealth, or apparent wealth throughout the western world for over three centuries. The involvement of the state in producing bank notes came with the creation of the Bank of England in 1694, which allowed for the issuance of these bank notes to facilitate payments-- in other words, paper money.

As mentioned earlier, Americans almost without exception wanted more and more credit to go about doing all of the amazing things that would eventually make the U.S. a world superpower. During the colonial era, British officials often complained, though, about the amount of paper money being emitted by various local banks. Other investors also noted the fundamental unsoundness of the banks issuing paper dollars. Still, Americans found paper money quite useful- they even used it to finance their Revolution. Printing too much "Continental Currency" was the only way a bankrupt Revolutionary government could keep the war effort going. But, once again, there was a cost. There were too many notes chasing too few goods, and the paper money collapsed. After this monetary disaster, those who drafted the U.S. Constitution mandated that only gold and silver should be money (I realize the Constitution is nothing more than a sheet of paper to many present-day politicians, but it can't hurt to understand the document's history.)

Nonetheless, Americans continued to be tempted by banking. After all they wanted loans to do all of the things that they had not saved up enough real money to do. In the first years of the republic, Secretary of the Treasury Alexander Hamilton managed to get Congress to approve the Bank of the United States- something akin to a central bank that would attempt to regulate subordinate banks. Over the course of the next 120 years, there would be repeated complaints about central banking, most famously by Andrew Jackson, who managed to kill the Bank of the US briefly, but the desire for a stronger central bank re-emerged after the Civil War.[2]

By the time of yet another banking panic in 1907, there were calls for "reform" in the banking system (please note the quotation marks around reform). Many of these reformers, like Carter Glass and William Jennings Bryan saw themselves as men of the people who wanted more oversight for what they saw as a chaotic banking system too tightly controlled by Wall Street. They hoped that the business cycle, the ups and downs of credit expansion and contraction, could somehow be smoothed over or regulated. At the same time they hoped that by creating a system with various branches throughout the country, that somehow the "money power" would be lessened or democratized.

However, it proved impossible to create a new stronger banking system that was somehow not centralized. Or more accurately, banking and corporate interests proved impossible to restrain in their desire for more concentration of global finance. The reality in 1913 was the creation of a powerful new central bank, the Federal Reserve, which issued the American nation's currency, and which is more or less independent of the U.S. government (even though there is some token Congressional oversight.)

One of the important themes, then, regarding banking in the Anglo-American world is the inability of people to stop larger and larger concentrations of banking power. You could say this is all a conspiracy, but the reality is that local control, or too much decentralization, can easily lead to chaos. If you think about the economy as a fragile entity easily spooked by exogenous crises, wouldn't you be tempted to only want your banking system backed up the taxing and military power of the most powerful nation on earth? This is not to say there weren't plenty of critics of the Federal Reserve System- but many of these critics simply wanted the central bank under the control of the federal government, which may or may not have changed the way the central bank operated. The power to create money and extend credit is a powerful force that corrupts and tempts many, whether they are in Wall Street or Washington, D.C.

The Faustian Bargain of Central Banking (and planning)

Put another way, if people wanted banking, they were possibly going to have to put up with the bankers getting to make the rules. Much of the modern history of banking- like the history of larger and larger concentrations of corporate power- can be seen as a kind of deal with the devil. It reminds me of what several colonial Americans used to say about civil liberties, or how those who would give up their liberties for security deserve neither. I think the same can be said regarding those who chose to give economic power over to large banks or other monopolies in the modern capitalist system. When you relinquish self-reliance in order to create a wealthier economy, perhaps you end up with neither.

Obviously, we have not reached a point where large numbers of people will honestly wish for a return to the early nineteenth century. That was a period of backbreaking labor, of widespread disease, and it was an era where you had to provide your own defense against social unrest.

But people need to remember that there are downsides to our increasingly inter-connected world, highly dependent upon "complex systems" for survival. When you don't grow your own food, when you rely on large bureaucracies to provide basic services, when you don't heat your own home, and when all of your wealth is simply on a computer screen somewhere that can be visible to practically anyone (especially the government), you are vulnerable in more ways than one.

Without denying the progress that has been made in the past century, you need to remember that every economic or political system has its downside. Metals like gold and silver provide one example among many of ways in which you might try to insure yourself against systemic collapse.

A Short History of the American Dollar: Doubling Down On Debt

Another important theme to remember is that the desire among Americans to have easy money and cheap credit goes back to the founding of the colonies. The faustian bargain that I spoke of can easily be seen in the history of the dollar, a history of more and more Americans wanting fewer and fewer tangible checks on the borrowing and spending power of individuals or the government. What we currently call "fiat money," meaning paper money that is not backed by any attachment to gold or silver and decreed money by the state, actually has its roots far back in the American past. Americans- along with their bankers- have often been tempted by the idea that you don't need to pay for things in the present, and that money can in fact be conjured out of thin air.

Beginning in the 1690s, and starting in Massachusetts, several colonies began to print paper notes, initially with the intention of making them convertible into gold or silver as a way of generating confidence in the notes among the public. But in nearly every case, convertibility stopped quickly, as it was revealed that the colonies had neither the tax revenue nor the specie (gold and silver) to back the notes they created. By 1740 most colonies had watched their paper notes--usually referred to as "dollars"--devalue against gold by anywhere from 80 to 99%! Yes, an early and bitter lesson in unconvertible currency- but one to be repeated many, many times. The temptation to take on more debt, or to create more loans than could be backed by specie (gold or silver) never went away for long. Over the course of the eighteenth century, there would be experiments with so-called "land banks" that also issued bank notes not backed by specie—most failed in a matter of years, if not months. But many Americans, be they poor farmers, or larger land speculators, were addicted to debt, and constantly hoped that they could somehow avoid the discipline imposed by a gold or silver standard.

I already mentioned the catastrophe of the Continental Dollar, which lost nearly all of its value during the American Revolution. This catastrophe did inspire the authors of the Constitution to mandate that no state should be able to emit paper money, and the document demanded that only gold and silver coin should be legal tender for payment of debts. Congress alone would have the power "to coin money, [and to] regulate the value thereof, and of foreign coin," in Article I, section 8 of the Constitution. Acting on this authority, Congress passed the Coinage Act in 1792 which defined the dollar as a weight of 371.25 grains of pure silver and/or a weight of 24.75 grains of pure gold- a bimetallic standard.[3]

However, old habits died hard. Within three years of the passing of the Constitution, Congress also authorized the creation of the Bank of United States, which would issue dollar denominated bank notes that were supposed to be fully redeemable by their holders in gold or silver on demand. This would soon lead to an explosion of commercial banks issuing more and more paper, backed by less and less gold or silver.

It wouldn't be long before some sort of crisis over convertibility would rear its ugly head yet again. With the country facing a war and in need of supplies, the Federal Government allowed a doubling of bank corporations from 117 to 212 in four years between 1811 and 1815. This was in addition to some 35 private unincorporated banks. The number of banknotes proliferated. At the time, there would be a need to have "money brokers" who were knowledgeable in the solvency of each of the hundreds of banks putting out paper money. Why was this? Because in 1814, the federal government allowed the private banks to stop converting bank notes into gold and silver due to a lack of specie. And this fateful decision meant that the Federal government would allow banks to renege on their contractual obligation to redeem bank notes in gold and silver in the future. With this precedent set, wildcat banking exploded in the period from 1815 up until the Civil War. And there were several episodes where banks stopped redeeming dollar notes in gold and silver: during the panics of 1819, 1837, and 1857, most banknotes in the U.S. could not be exchanged into precious metal. This also led to huge premiums being paid for gold and silver, as people scrambled for real money.[4]

Then came the Civil War. As most readers understand by now, governments can't finance wars without massive amounts of debt. This fact certainly applied to both the Union and to the Confederacy when war broke out in 1861. In the case of the Confederacy, their "dollars" became literally worthless by 1864 (many are worth far more now as collectors' items than in 1865). For the victorious Union, things didn't get that bad but the "dollar" was again trashed in the 1860s. Beginning in 1862, Congress established the

Greenback dollar in order to help fund war debts, and this dollar could not be converted into gold or silver. The United States would not return to convertibility until 1879. Meanwhile, when bankers or other merchants began to aggressively bid up the price of gold, the Union tried various schemes (including a stamp tax) to retard gold "speculation." None of it worked, of course, and at its lowest point, the Greenback lost nearly 70% of its value against gold.[5]

After the war, one "Mrs. Hepburn" challenged the constitutionality of a lower court ruling which had denied that her debt (to a certain Henry Griswold) could be paid with Greenbacks. The *Hepburn v. Griswold* case reached the Supreme Court in 1867, where in fact the judges denounced the actions of the Lincoln government and denied that Greenbacks dollars were legal tender. The Federal Government was not pleased, and neither were many railroads which had racked up large debts that could be paid more easily in the depreciated paper. And so by 1871, the composition of the court had changed as did the law: in *Knox v Le*e, the court reversed itself and held that fiat paper money was consistent (somehow) with the Constitution.[6]

As mentioned above, the Federal Reserve came into existence to supposedly lessen the frequency of banking panics. For twenty years, Federal Reserve notes were convertible into gold by American citizens. But the Federal Reserve had played a hand in suppressing interest rates and in creating the illusion of a gold standard by allowing Britain to rack up large debts during the 1920s. A spectacular boom and then bust occurred in 1929, even as the Federal Reserve supposedly existed to stop such excesses. One suggested solution to the depression brought on by debt was essentially more debt and dollar devaluation. In 1933, in the midst of the Depression, President Roosevelt ended the convertibility of Federal Reserve Notes into gold for U.S. citizens. In fact, he made private ownership of gold bullion illegal, even as many Americans refused to comply with the law. All European nations also went off the gold standard in 1936 as the western world slipped into renewed warfare.

By 1944, with the U.S. emerging from World War II as the last western power standing, the Bretton Woods system effectively made the U.S. dollar "good as gold," which meant that foreigners could exchange their dollars for gold, and no currency was allowed to rise or fall by more than one percent. This arrangement worked for nearly twenty years-until the 1960s, when the United States had racked up enough debt as to cause concern among foreigners regarding the overinflated value of the U.S. dollar.[7]

Another event during this time was the rising market price of silver. Since the 1870s, the market price of silver had crashed far below its monetary amount in terms of bullion content. But that was changing in the 1960s. By 1964, it was no longer economical for the U.S to coin silver, and by 1968 the last of the (reduced) silver coins were produced. 1964 also saw the end of silver certificates- where Americans could exchange one or five dollar bills for silver coins. Meanwhile, inflation and indebtedness also meant a rising gold price. By 1963, the market price of gold began to inch above the fixed value of 35 dollars, and eventually, by the summer of 1971, foreigners began to drain the U.S. of gold. Finally, on August 15, 1971, President Nixon ended the last vestiges of the gold backing to dollars, by closing the gold window to foreign banks. The United States- and soon much of the rest of the world- would be on a purely fiat currency standard. Gold and silver seemed to be irrelevant.[8]

The dream of those Americans who had issued unconvertible paper dollars as early as the 1690s had now become reality. Finally, American governments and banks need not be checked by any sort of attachment to a finite resource when making loans or when taking on debt. And if the banking system got into trouble infinite amounts of fiat money could be created to keep the confidence game going. As mentioned above, it really seems as though debt and deficits just don't matter anymore. They can be waived away in our modern world.

I want to remind you, the reader, of a very important point in my opinion. And it is that the money used by a society is a reflection of the values of that society. In our case, digital or electronic money says to me that work doesn't matter, it says that actually having resources to trade for money are irrelevant, and it shows that people should trust the almighty power of the state to take care of everything, since unpleasant realities like saving for the future or looking after oneself with your own resources have become irrelevant. We either live in a utopia, or in a nightmare, since money can just be typed up on a computer screen (and banks can be re-liquified in the same manner.)

Many will insist that we will never reach a point where confidence in our monetary and financial system could only be restored by a return to some sort of tangible backing for our money. They seem to believe that the confidence game of endless consumption is intact, and that the world can continue to rack up debt without consequences. They will say that we live in a new economy, a new world, and that gold and silver are vestiges of a bygone era. Why worry about taking care of yourself? The state will do that. Why worry about finite resources? They will magically appear. The business cycle? We can repeal that too. Some might even say that our leaders in government and finance know better than to repeat the mistakes of the past when it comes to printing too much money and driving the value of the currency into the ground.

As a response to these unrealistic hopes and assumptions, I will trot out the oft-used (but not often followed) advice of George Bernard Shaw: "You have a choice between the natural stability of gold and the honesty and intelligence of the members of government. And with all due respect for those gentlemen, I advise you, as long as the capitalist system lasts, vote for gold."[9]

The Problem with Conventional Financial Advice

Given the fact that crises of confidence or banking panics (or depressions) are a fact of economic life for modern earthlings, you would think that most financial advisors would at least recommend some sort of reasonable allocation (10-30%) to the precious metals sector, either in bullion form, or with mining shares. You might think so, but you would be wrong. Well-known contrarian investor Marc Faber reported in 2011 how most hedge fund managers at a conference admitted to him they did not own one ounce of gold (I find that a little hard to believe, but on second thought, maybe not.)[10] In fact, investment managers not only fail to recommend a decent allocation to precious metals, but as a rule they deny that precious metals are a distinct asset class from other commodity investments in the first place! To me, this borders on tragic.

I mentioned earlier that, in addition to teaching history, that I also hold a real estate license. There are many similarities between realtors and financial planners. Both are supposed to give advice, but both are also interested in making sales. Obviously, this is a conflict of interest. On the other hand, in an ideal world, anyone dispensing financial advice should want to get their facts straight and be seen as credible—in the long run this should work to help you win over clients. For example, would you use a realtor again who advised you to borrow five times your income with zero percent down for a house in 2005 that subsequently lost 65% of its value? It seems to me that anyone involved in dispensing financial advice needs to understand that their credibility is on the line when they make recommendations that continue to fall short of expectations. Recommendations like "stocks for the long run" when stock indexes (and even individual companies) have a history of going nowhere for long periods of time don't build lasting client relationships. Conversely, when a financial planner denigrates or ignores the role of genuine, tangible assets in a portfolio, you may want to look for the door.

So many commentators say that the precious metals are in a bubble, and, of course, that they don't own it (or so they say). I would remind them that perception is reality with all "investments"- many of which are simply numbers on a computer screen. These commentators will tell you with a straight face that stocks are the way to make money off of new industries, new technologies- ignoring the fact that most investors made no money in the last decade, even while CEOs made off like bandits. They also ignore the fact that stock markets in Germany and Japan in the 1940s more or less went to 0, even while people needed tangible assets, whether oil, liquor, or metals. Stocks are no replacement for tangible assets.

Fiat Currency in Extremis: Going Back to a World of Barter?

I am not necessarily trying to scare anyone, either. Buying gold and silver does not necessarily mean that you think the world is about to end. The world did not end in the 1970s, when many people made fortunes off of gold and silver investments. But playing the game of investing and speculating means correctly understanding the risks you face from irresponsible, corrupt governments waging war on savers. There have been several examples around the world of monetary and political authorities taking the easy way out by simply debasing their currency when faced with the inconvenience of fiscal insolvency. The results, in some cases, have been horrific.

In recent years, one of the most tragic examples of this kind of monetary irresponsibility can be seen in Zimbabwe. The suffering of the people of this African nation is unimaginable, all the more so when you consider that the government blocks sufficient news coverage of the plight of the people of Zimbabwe. The case of Zimbabwe demonstrates the logic of fiat currency in extremis: a corrupt and abusive state arrogates total power to itself, destroys private property, and defines what money is- the public be damned. The regime of Robert Mugabe, particularly between 2002 and 2009, reduced the people to scraping for gold in the ground because the paper currency became worthless- an important reminder regarding what will and will not be money when times get tough. For many of the former landholders living under a regime so tone deaf to the right of private property, there are only two options left for survival: revolt or flee.

I understand that the United States is far removed from the plight of Zimbabwe. But I also understand that when their backs are to the wall, policy elites will do whatever is necessary to save themselves—are you as a saver really going to assume that other people have your best interests at heart? Perhaps you need another example of monetary incompetence and corruption: Weimar Germany. In the 1920s, after having been defeated in World War I- a war that the state paid for with borrowing, not with taxes- the government simply continued the same profligate policies in peacetime. Some have claimed this was some sort of ploy not to pay war indemnities to other nations, even though the indemnities could not be paid in rapidly depreciating German marks. What historians do agree upon, though, is that governments, once addicted to irresponsible monetary policies, do not heed warning signs and are perfectly happy running the currency and the country into the ground. As proof of this, scholars point to the central banker of Weimar Germany, Rudolph Havenstein, the man who oversaw the complete destruction of the Reichmark (where a Reichmark had been valued in the single digits to a U.S dollar, under Havenstein, it was valued in the trillions). For his part, though, Havenstein maintained throughout the entire episode that there was no connection between the supply of money being created and price levels of exchange rates. This bears repeating: the man who destroyed the Reichmark claimed there was no connection between the supply of money and price levels![11]

The Weimar and Zimbabwe cases are among the more extreme examples of monetary debasement. But there have been other, less dramatic examples of high inflation that still did real damage to savers. When I was in graduate school, I met students from countries like Turkey and Argentina, who had both seen serious episodes of inflation during their lifetimes. Both understood the power of inflation (the friend from Turkey once commented in wonder that he never believed prices could actually go down until he came to the U.S; we'll see about that in the future.) The case of Argentine devaluation was well-publicized, and may also be a meaningful comparison about what could happen someday to the United States and its dollar. As recently as 2001 not only was the Argentine peso devalued because of the nation's insolvency, but Argentines who held accounts in dollars had those accounts forcible reconverted into the greatly devalued peso. In fact in many cases, Argentines were prevented from withdrawing too much cash from ATM machines!! Keep this in mind next time you think that cash or short-term deposits are "safe investments."

Economists are civil servants and monetary authorities are not gods. This should be the lesson taken from Zimbabwe, Argentina, or Weimar Germany. I should also add that many financial professionals and financial media outlets are often influenced by the financial interests representing Wall Street generally. It is not their job to focus their clients' attention on the financial mishaps which can so often befall even the strongest of nations.

History versus Economics

At the risk of being impolite, I would actually refer to most economists as simply academic spokesmen for the banking cartel that runs the modern credit-based monetary system. I say this in the spirit of realism. Cartels and well-connected elites have always run the world: it is no different today, in many respects, than it ever was. So is it a surprise that these cartels need the intellectual respectability conferred by universities and academic think tanks? Of course economists, at least publicly, will never admit to being apparatchiks for banking elites. The problem with economists is that they actually believe that what they preach constitute natural laws, or that what they postulate comes close to scientific truth. This is very dangerous, as I mentioned above in the case of Rudolph Havenstein. It can also be seen in statements made by Federal Reserve heads like Alan Greenspan and Ben Bernanke when the former pronounced derivatives as creating a safer market, and when the latter claimed that home prices would always remain relatively stable.[12]

Whether or not you doubt the sincerity of men like Bernanke or Greenspan, there are too many examples from monetary history of elites hiding the truth about a nation's fundamental fiscal solvency to always trust these leaders. The power of history enables people to remember facts and experiences from distant eras, experiences that stand outside of most people's lifetimes. Monetary history also demonstrates the indeterminacy, even irrationality of human action and behavior, something which cuts against the more hubristic assumptions of the modern monetary high priests called economists. But again, would you expect anyone who benefits from the status quo to go out of their way to tell you the truth?

There have also been numerous examples of companies in bed with the government being able to pull off some astounding feats of fraud in recent years. A notable example can be seen with the case of the MF Global brokerage firm; a firm that clearly stole client funds and was able to get away with it. (If you don't believe me, just google "MF Global Client Accounts" and see what turns up.) Many of these clients are still waiting for their money, still waiting to be made whole. Unfortunately, this financial atrocity (yes, that is what I would call it) should remind every thinking adult that bad things happen to good people. Are you so sure you can afford to leave all of your money in a bank or in a brokerage account? I say no. I think that you need to understand to have all of your bases covered when it comes to insuring your financial future. If you have been watching these financial calamities over the past several years, and you still don't understand the need to diversify your assets, I think you are doing a pretty poor job of risk management.

But I am fairly certain that as we continue to experience more confidence-shattering episodes of financial fraud, whether it be along the lines of subprime fraud, another Madoff Ponzi scheme, an MF Global, or bank holidays or brokerage account seizures, more and more people will experience the kind of conversion experience that I have written about above.

And it is quite likely that the public (or at least a significant chunk of the public) will buy gold and silver not for a quick profit, not to try to game the system, and not because they want to buy more SUVs or McMansions in the U.S. Instead, they will buy precious metals out of a sense of moral imperative. This is where the game changes. This, I believe, is the most powerful motivation to purchase something, and it has the power to launch the price of silver to the moon.

"He Who Has The Gold Makes The Rules": Silver Taking the Lead from Her More Powerful, Yellow Elder Sibling

Although this is a book about silver, it is impossible to talk about silver without talking about gold-- especially because gold is the only precious metal that is in any sense still "monetized" by governments. What I mean by this is that central banks still hold gold as a reserve asset. Gold is still officially seen as a form of savings by those who run the world (or try to) even as they are often reticent about why they own and acquire this metal. Central banks may also be embarrassed that between 1975 and 2005, they dumped around 5,000 tonnes of gold, or roughly 150 million ounces of gold on the market. (1 tonne equals 32,000 ounces of gold; 1,000 tonnes is 32 million ounces). The behavior of central banks over the last 30 years might have encouraged people to believe that gold was a barbarous relic after all. But I bet these banks privately had a conversion on the road to Damascus regarding gold sometime around the failure of Lehman Brothers in the fall of 2008.

And so now, not only have central banks stopped selling gold, but as a group they are *buying* gold. Please note that these are usually central banks outside the United States and Europe, but these are the countries who are the creditor nations in today's global economy. In 2011, central banks purchased nearly 100 more tonnes of gold than they sold. This is the third year in a row this has happened, and it signals a momentous sea change in the gold market. On the demand side, it looks like most people who sought to scrap old gold jewelry have done it, or at the very least that the desire of private holders of gold to sell is also diminishing. The World Gold Council, reported in 2011 that for the third year in a row, gold recycling fell, to around 1200 tonnes globally.[13]

So how much gold might the central banks of the world be looking to buy? It could be quite a lot, as many, many countries have miniscule amounts of gold under their control, at least according to the World Gold Council. In fact, a majority of countries in the world have less than 10% of their foreign currency reserves in gold and FIFTY (50) countries have on average 1.5% of their reserves in gold. It really makes you wonder why banks don't just go ahead and continue to sell off all of their gold, since it is such a small amount. But they aren't selling: instead, they are big buyers. The countries that average less than 1.5% of reserves in gold include such large economies as China, Japan, Taiwan, Saudi Arabia, Brazil, Hong Kong, Indonesia, Canada, Mexico, and Chile, among many others. These banks, in order to simply increase the percentage of their holdings to 5%, would probably be on the market for close to 10,000 tonnes of gold, which is roughly four years of global gold production! And this could be a conservative estimate. Some would argue that China alone could buy 10,000 tonnes of gold on its own, particularly as their currency reserves continue to increase.[14]

Many who follow the gold and silver market understand the historic and cultural importance both monetary metals have held in India. Indians import sizable sums of both metals from foreigners. But China is giving India a run for its money in terms of precious metal accumulation. China is an absolutely essential part of the story both for gold and for silver. For over 60 years, the Chinese people were more or less banned from owning gold and silver by its communist government. But with the change in leadership in China, in addition to the aftershocks of the 2008 financial crisis, two important things have happened. First off, you have Chinese officials openly criticizing the dollar reserve system, and this government has, in small ways, already begun to reduce dollar holdings among their reserves. And second, the Chinese are not only allowing their citizens to own gold and silver as an inflation hedge, but actually encouraging it. You read this correctly: far from disparaging gold and silver, the Chinese government is encouraging these investments as diversifiers in individual portfolios. In recent months and years, Chinese investment in gold and silver has soared. If you are reading this book in the United States, this may surprise you. In at least one very large country in the world, the government is warning its citizens of exactly the kinds of things I am warning you about, and defending the need for savers to own the monetary metals.[15]

What Are Savers To Do?

You would do well to listen to the investment advice being given by the Chinese government to savers, much abused savers, as far as I'm concerned. In the United States and throughout the western world, savers are being stiffed with 0% interest rates. A truly unprecedented phenomenon. Savers have to understand, as I wrote above, that they have been turned into speculators, assuming they care about trying to grow their money in this economic environment. The desire for self-respect ought to lead average people to do things that may at first glance appear to be unconventional, but upon more reflection simply represent doing something pretty smart in the long run. For savers/speculators in this environment, a challenge has been raised. Are you up to it?

Chapter 3
Silver, the Blogosphere, and the Turn Toward Realism

Trying to get at the truth, to honestly look oneself in the mirror isn't easy. And I don't want to sound like I have a monopoly on honesty, either. But one of the more annoying aspects of our current financial or political system is people's inability to see the world for what it is. People often like to overlook the nastier, less pleasant sides of how nations are created, how power is maintained, and how little people are more often than not abused, lied to, and manipulated by those who craft public opinion.

In the aftermath of the crisis of 2008, investors should have learned something very important about our financial system: the people who are "in charge" are not able to avert a crisis. Even if the Lords of Finance cared about you and wanted to help you, the truth is they are often powerless against this force of nature called the market. Central banks often simply react to messes once they occur. In many ways, you are on your own. But I'm not sure everyone learned this, and I'm pretty sure that not everyone is investing with an eye to protect themselves against the kinds of financial accidents described in this book.

Still, the word about gold and silver is getting out in one very important way with the help of the blogosphere.

There are a number of sites where people like me can find common cause with others when it comes to alternative investing and thinking in general. The internet revolution, or what has also been likened to the Protestant Reformation in terms of the democratization of knowledge, allows for a more honest assessment of the dominant memes, or narrative of reality spread by the establishment media. Put another way, the internet has allowed for the tangible asset worldview to get some sort of fair hearing.

I've tried to compile a list at the end of this chapter (apologies to anyone left out) of the various sites that have influenced those of us who buy silver as an investment. Over the last three or four years, whenever I would go onto any number of sites, whether it was zerohedge.com, jessescrossroadscafe.com, jsmineset.com, kereport.com, or others, I felt part of a community of dissidents. Not that they were all the same, or all in agreement, but in my mind they represented a distinct worldview challenging conventional assumptions about markets, money, and politics. It might not be too much to think of these sites as an investment underground. And so just as people have been moving toward alternative investments over the course of the last several years, they are also looking at alternative sources for information.

As has been said, the "revolution will not be televised," and since markets express these kinds of social changes, the internet reformation, a reformation in the diffusion of knowledge, has the capacity to radically alter people's understanding regarding where to put their money. This internet transformation was not available to people in the 1970s, the last time that we had a mania in gold, silver, and mining shares. The internet may play an important role in reintroducing the monetary metals to the global financial system. The internet may also play a role in helping average people to reorder their lives and to more accurately assess what to expect from the economy in the future.

Kenneth Parsons, the proprietor of the silverbearcafe since 2001, summarized well the standard complaints of the alternative media against the modern-day "monied power" who:

"...elect whomever they want locally and nationally, and never expose the crooked money system. They promote school bonds, expensive and detrimental farm programs, "urban renewal," foreign aid, and many other schemes which place the people more deeply in debt to the bankers. Thoughtful citizens wonder why billions are spent on one program and billions on another which may duplicate it or even nullify it, such as paying some farmers not to raise crops, while at the same time building dams or canals to irrigate more farm land. Crazy or stupid?

Neither. The goal is more debt. Thousands of government-sponsored methods of wasting money go on continually. Most make no sense, but they are never exposed for what they really are: siphons sucking our Nation's economic lifeblood."[1]

Parsons, like many of the other alternative media editors supportive of silver felt that it would not be a crisis if borrowers defaulted, or if banks went under. For example, take a nation like Iceland: they went through a nasty crash by allowing banks to fail, and, while painful, it was not the end of the world. Their economy is now on stronger footing.

Monopolies choking off the lifeblood of innovation are not popular in good times, even less so in bad. Whether or not you agree with all of the views of someone like Parsons (who also does not believe the government view of 9/11, for example), you have to admit that oftentimes it is true how the insiders are the protected ones. Maybe they are government bureaucrats, maybe they are bankers, maybe they work for the UN, or IMF, maybe they are protected in some way by elite connections or wealth. I mentioned earlier how as the economy continues to downsize, as people become more sensitive to the yawning gap between the success of the well-connected and the challenges facing everyone else, what historians call the "anti-monopolist" worldview will continue to gain favor.

It is also the case that anger over elite privilege is nothing new. Bloggers like Parsons are simply reiterating views from over 150 years earlier, such as those of President Andrew Jackson, who, when he destroyed the Bank of the United States, famously said:

"I too have been a close observer of the doings of the Bank of the United States. I have had men watching you for a long time, and am convinced that you have used the funds of the bank to speculate in the breadstuffs of the country. When you won, you divided the profits amongst you, and when you lost, you charged it to the Bank...You are a den of vipers and thieves. I have determined to rout you out and, by the Eternal, I will rout you out."[2]

The present-day generation is now having to live with the deleterious consequences of modern credit and banking systems. I likened these systems earlier to nuclear power; yes there are great benefits, but you need to always beware about their downside.

While not all of the following individuals in this chapter are in agreement with more extreme elements of the anti-monopolist worldview, most of the more high-profile silver bulls agree with some of the anti-authoritarian or anti-banking sentiments laid out above. Here are a few of the more influential silver analysts or investors who have helped share the silver story with likely a few million listeners or readers over the last 15 years.

Ted Butler
butlerresearch.com

As detailed earlier, the COMEX division of the New York Mercantile Exchange leads the world in the pricing of silver bullion. The institution does possess more silver than any other exchange, although what it possesses is only a fraction (30-100 million ounces) of the more than 1 billion ounces of bullion on the planet.

More than any other analyst, Ted Butler has focused the attention of precious metals investors on the actions of traders at the COMEX with his analysis of The Commitment of Traders Report (COT), an accounting of the positions (long or short) of those who speculate with paper silver. Butler reminds people of the power of the COMEX exchange in setting the price of silver. Mr. Butler maintains that the price of silver has suffered from a manipulative short side concentration. A manipulative short side concentration means that the large banks who are selling paper silver are in a position to rig prices lower, and to trick enough other players (who are often nothing more than computers) into selling. These large banks make money by being short, then they are able to make money again by going long (buying positions) and riding silver back up to levels from which they previously sold.

For his part, Butler was turned on to the silver manipulation argument way back in the 1980s by a brokerage client of his, Izzy Friedman. Friedman challenged Butler to explain how a metal that was in chronic deficit still suffered from price declines. Remember that for nearly two decades, industrial silver demand could not be met from mine supply—it had to be met from the depletion of above ground stockpiles. During most of that period, according to the CPM Group, investors were selling silver, and yet the market was still in deficit. Making matters worse, investor dishoarding could not stop the need for silver stockpiles to be consumed by industrial uses. Ted slowly came to the conclusion that such an extreme situation could only occur in an environment where markets aren't free, where there was some sort of price capping going on. But at a time when there were no longer legal restrictions on the ownership of silver bullion, it was hard to see how there was any official capping of the silver price from the government. Instead, Ted began to look at the behavior of futures traders at the largest futures exchange for silver, the COMEX division of the New York mercantile exchange. It was there that Ted unearthed a large commercial short position in silver.

Ted believed that this concentrated position was in violation of commodity law. And back in 1985, Butler approached everyone from mining executives to members of the Commodity Futures Trading Commission (CFTC) about it. To his surprise, these people all scoffed at the notion that there was manipulation in the silver market. Some would undoubtedly say that concentrations existed in other commodities, or that it was impossible to know how a certain entity was or was not hedged in the physical market. These explanations left much to be desired. Silver is not just another easily extracted commodity, and it was not a commodity whose stockpiles could be easily replaced. The short concentration made up at least 20% or more of global production, and nearly half of all bullion stockpiles at the time-- numbers which far exceeded the concentrations in other commodities. And none of the firms involved were miners who somehow needed to legitimately hedge their production.

Over time, Ted stopped trying to convince people about the manipulation. Investors ignored silver in the 1990s, and the price not only languished, but actually made new lows toward the end of the decade. Still, Ted's attraction to the silver story never went away, and he once again began to write about silver, this time for the clients of James Cook, the President of Investment Rarities. Many of these articles about the silver market soon made their way to the internet, and some were later published as a book, *Silver Profits in the New Century*. With this new exposure, thousands of people began to understand many unique aspects of the silver market. Many began to buy silver by the ton.

Butler now publishes a newsletter devoted to the silver market, where he provides detailed analysis of the movements in the COT report, as well as many other aspects of the silver market. The consistent theme of these reports has been the size of the net short position held by the four largest banks at the COMEX. Over the last several years, the size of the net short position has declined somewhat, from over 200 million ounces to closer to 150 million ounces as of June 2012. At 200 million ounces of silver, the four largest banks have been net short over 20% of global mine production. Depending on whose numbers you use, this net short position is either 20% of all silver bullion on the planet, or about 10% of all above ground silver bars and coins believed to be on planet Earth. To contrast this with gold, the net short position of the largest four traders equals only 15 million ounces, or less than 1 percent of the 3 billion ounces of gold bullion in the world, and less than 18 percent of global gold production.[3]

Some may point out (correctly) that concentrations exist in many commodity markets. In our age of large multinational corporations and banks, it is not surprising

73

that a few, large players dominate trading in many futures markets. In the case of orange juice futures, for example, four traders hold over 60% of the net short position in that market (as of the spring of 2012). But this concentration still only amounts to around 240 million pounds of orange juice out of the 55 billion pounds of annual production (less than 1%). In the case of light sweet crude oil, there have been long concentrations at over 20% of all open interest, but this only amounts to at most 300 million barrels of oil out of the over 10 billion barrels produced annually, (or roughly 3%). In terms of oil stockpiles, which stand at over 4 billion barrels as of 2011, the short concentration is less than 9% of oil stockpiles.[4]

So, perspective counts, and the concentrated net short position in silver is far worse than that seen in other commodities.

Through his newsletter service, Ted Butler has encouraged thousands of investors to protest behavior at the COMEX that he sees as manipulative to the price of silver. Why should large banks be able to "sell" 20% of global production short? Why would anyone need to hedge this much silver (meaning locking in a price now for future delivery)? In response, over 12,000 individuals have left public comments with the CFTC regarding the need for position limits in the silver market. Most of these comments have called for limiting any one entity to 1500 contracts (each contract is 5000 silver ounces). Importantly, few if any comments posted by the public referred to the need for position limits in any other commodity besides silver, as of 2011.

For a man who was largely ignored in the 1980s when he approached the CFTC regarding the need for better regulations in the commodity markets, the fact that a commission of the CFTC has responded to Ted Butler represents a major achievement- whether or not any action takes place. Butler's petition campaign is also largely the reason for this, since in no other market than silver has the public commentary been so large. By August 2011, Commissioner Bart Chilton acknowledged an ongoing investigation into several unusual trading practices in the silver market, particularly the 12% takedown in price within minutes, late on a Sunday night, May 1, 2011.

These kinds of short selling crashes in the futures markets, which often occur in a matter of minutes, are likely not about economical selling, by which I mean someone trying to get the best price for what they have to sell. How could they be? If you are trying to sell a large position you would want to do it slowly, so as not to hurt yourself in the sale (in other words you need more time than a few minutes to find willing buyers for the large sell orders you are dumping on the market.) The price smash in May of 2011 (followed by another one in September 2011) often occurred during the electronic, "after hours" trading session, when liquidity is even smaller than during regular market hours. Commissioner Chilton is on record criticizing the role of High Frequency Trading in creating this price smash. Chilton goes so far as to refer to High Frequency traders as "cheetahs." He has said that "cheetah" trading is "parasitical" and he questions how much, if any, value these traders add to any given market in which they participate. Chilton also hopes that additional financial reform will regulate the High Frequency Traders, even as he acknowledges the recent Dodd Frank bill does not do so. However, as of 2012, little has changed regarding the regulation either of concentrated positions in the silver market, or regarding the position size of the shorts in this market.[5]

As far as Ted Butler is concerned, however, he has maintained that it is the responsibility of those who regulate futures markets to stop large banks or traders from being able to control a market, or to pick on smaller traders at an institution as important as the COMEX. In addition, the mispricing of an important asset like silver will eventually have deleterious consequences. Remember what I wrote above regarding the silver deficit and how silver stockpiles dropped over 90% from 1970 to 2000. Butler blames market inefficiencies, like the paper pricing of silver, for this drop.

In the end, however, Butler believes that there will come a time when those entities that are short the metal will be stranded or otherwise forced to cover, thus driving the price much higher. These entities are not invincible. If enough people took physical delivery of metal, the price of silver could soar by many times.

Butler's weekly reports are available as part of a subscription service, through butlerresearch.com However, Ed Steer, of Casey Research, often closely follows Butler's work, and you can sometimes find authorized, free excerpts from Butler's work on Steer's website. (Casey Research, founded by Doug Casey is in general a great resource for all things gold and silver related, by the way.)[6]

David Morgan
silver-investor.com

During the internet boom in the late 1990s, while everybody else was focusing on the newest, hottest tech stock, a lonely voice in the wilderness decided to establish a site devoted to silver investing. At the time, I am certain that most people could have cared less: silver had been in the dumps for years, having fallen over 90% from its intraday peak of 50 dollars in 1980. On the other hand, the late-1990s was the time when Warren Buffet decided to buy over 130 million ounces of the metal, so David was in good company. But the retail crowd was still years away from buying the white metal in any large amount. Silver at the time was trading at the lowest inflation adjusted price in centuries-likely even lower than the 26 cent market price of 1932- due to the incredible increases in the monetary base after the US went off any semblance of a gold standard in 1971.

And so, beginning in 1997, David began releasing "The Morgan Report" newsletter on all things silver, in addition to launching the website silver-investor.com. Through these venues, David covers all aspects of silver investing: from the supply and demand dynamics, to political developments impacting silver, and – especially- silver mining stocks. Many of these mining stocks are up over 2000% since the lows of 2002. David can take credit for having produced some of the best investment returns in the stock market newsletter business. For example, he recommended to his subscribers that they buy shares in Minefinders and in Western Copper, both of which produced returns in excess of 1000%. Morgan will be the first to tell you that not all of his stocks have been winners, he will also be the first to tell you that mining stocks are by no means a substitute for real bullion.

By his own account, David was seduced by financial markets at the age of eleven. But he also shared a nagging concern about money, particularly after Lyndon Johnson fully demonetized silver by 1968. David recounted that when he asked his teacher why gold and silver were no longer legal tender in the U.S. he learned "that it snows indoors." People just aren't supposed to ask too many questions about the monetary system, or become too concerned about inflation and currency debasement. This experience in school eventually taught him an important lesson: learn to think for yourself.

For his part, Morgan absorbed information from the burgeoning number of books in the late 1960s and 1970s that did focus on currency debasement as well as on the monopoly powers of central banks. One book by Gary Allen, *None Dare Call It Conspiracy* laid out the case of the banking state's power in the modern world. This book was a forerunner of *The Creature from Jekyll Island*, by G. Edward Griffin, which makes similar points about the dangerous concentration of power represented by the Federal Reserve. From these books, and others- like Ayn Rand's *Atlas Shrugged*- David learned many of the basic tenets of what is popularly called Austrian economics: that inflation is in many ways immoral, and that an honest monetary system is the basis for an honest economy and society.

Throughout the 1970s, Morgan followed several of the best-known market newsletter writers, like Richard Russell, Jim Dines, Jim Sinclair, and Howard Ruff, hoping one day to follow in their footsteps. As of 2012, The Morgan Report has over 40,000 subscribers. David also recommends the newsletter, Independent Living, which seeks to educate people about the need to get off of the power grid and to become as self-reliant as possible.

After the launch of his website in 1997, David devoted a significant amount of time to travelling the world, attending various precious metals conferences where industry insiders, mining executives, and investors meet. He played an important role in the launching of the Silver Summit in 2002 in Spokane, Washington, which is one of the only conference venues devoted solely to silver investing. In 2006, he published *Get the Skinny on Silver Investing*, one of the few books at the time on silver. Over the past few years, Dave has been what many might call the face of the silver bulls, at least judging from his appearances on CNBC or Fox Business News, in addition to numerous other online financial news programs. He has also produced short videos for youtube describing his support for honest money.

David Morgan likes to sum up his philosophy on investing and life with these three sentences: "Buy Real, Get Real, Be Real." I think it is an important statement of the investing realism that many in today's financial system need to embrace

You can also find Morgan's "Ten Rules for Silver Investing" at his site, silver-investor.com.

Early on in his career as a silver analyst, Morgan became involved as a metals and mining analyst for Jim Puplava's finacialsense.com. Puplava gave Morgan access to thousands of listeners through financialsense.com.

Jim Puplava
financialsense.com

Jim Puplava established the Financialsense Newshour (FSN) in 1985, and later financialsense.com. As the founder of Puplava Financial Services Group, Puplava has been investing in silver for his clients since 2002, and has recommended the white metal to listeners of his program. However, Puplava is interested in more than just silver. This site and radio program feature a remarkable versatility in authors, including not only leading asset managers, or newsletter writers, but also historians, sociologists, and financial journalists. Puplava works hard to introduce his audience to all sorts of takes on economic events, and his editorial staff publishes articles from literally hundreds of other relatively unknown market commentators or journalists. The individual articles or radio interviews with Jim do not fit the short, superficial soundbite format of the mainstream media, either. To me, this is a refreshing change, even if it might not work with the shortened attention spans of many out there.

Early on in Puplava's career as an asset manager he—like countless others- endured the 1987 Crash. In the aftermath of the crash, Puplava tried to understand other ways to invest, and began to read the work of Austrian economists, as well as others who voiced a more bearish or concerned view of deficit spending, or who believed that sooner or later the reckless expansion of credit would have a nasty outcome. This early interest turned him on to gold, and Puplava has had positions in the metal and in mining stocks going back to the early 1990s. Then, through his association with Morgan, Puplava got into silver fairly near the bottom of its bear market, around 4 dollars. Puplava's interest in silver also led him and his firm to help finance mining companies Silver Standard and Aurelion Resources.

Puplava's interest in financial journalism dates back to the 1980s, but this interest did not always lead to fulfilling encounters with the conventional media. An early experience as a financial reporter at a local TV station in San Diego left him with more than a few bad impressions about the way established outlets cover the news. Once, Puplava had planned to do a report on the bad deals provided by car leases, only to find his story yanked at the last minute by the higher-ups because the story might offend one of the sponsors of the station. Jim was also disappointed at how many other news stories were filtered or ignored by the evening news for reasons not having to do with the merit of the story. The adversarial, entertainment-driven aspect of conventional news only further disappointed him. This is why Puplava struck out on his own, and taking advantage of the internet revolution, reached out to tens of thousands of listeners a month through both his radio program and website. An early article of his on the silver market, "Silver: The Undervalued Asset Looking For a Catalyst" was reportedly spread around the floor of the Chicago Mercantile Exchange at a time when silver was below 5 dollars an ounce.[7]

The efforts of Puplava and his team are not just about managing money, or assessing risk, or making speculative profits on hot stocks. Of course in this casino financial system of ours, there has to be room for educating savers regarding how to play in the casino. But Puplava is more concerned about warning people to be prepared, to brace for the coming storm. He is an expert on peak oil, and he has interviewed many who try to live off the grid as much as possible.

For someone who is an asset manager, it seems odd that so many of the articles on the site focus on things like a depression, or the need for tangible assets. But Puplava, like many other silver bulls, understands the need to stand apart from others when it comes to money and investing.

Franklin Sanders
the-moneychanger.com

       For the late Jim Blanchard, Sanders wrote one of the best known books on silver investing, *The Silver Bonanza*, at a moment in the early 1990s when few thought silver would ever regain its 1980 peak at 50 dollars. Many silver analysts are indebted to men like Sanders, Blanchard, and Jerome Smith for identifying the unique fundamentals which set up such astonishing potential for the silver price. By the 1980s, Sanders established a successful coin dealership, The Moneychanger, based in Tennessee. Sanders' free daily commentary on precious metals, as well as on other aspects of the financial markets can be found at the-moneychanger.com

       Sanders is one of the few precious metals dealers who recommends owning more silver than gold. He generally (depending on the state of the market at the time) recommends people put roughly 60-70% of their money into silver for three reasons. First, history shows that silver always accompanies gold in a bull market rise. Second, the smaller, more volatile silver market rises faster over the bull market's life, and markets usually end when sixteen or fewer ounces of silver buy one ounce of gold. (Compare 84 ounces to one as late as 2008.) Third, silver is money, and would be easiest to barter in a major currency accident. He recommends that Americans own the pre-1964 silver currency, first and foremost.

       Like many others in the bullion industry, Sanders is an unapologetic defender of individual rights and personal freedom. Unlike others, he has put his money where his mouth is on more than one occasion. In 1985 he started a gold and silver bank to offer an interface between the paper money and gold and silver money systems and legally and constitutionally to re-monetize gold and silver privately. Surprise -- IRS took offense, and in 1990 indicted him, his wife, and 25 others for conspiracy to delay the IRS in the performance of its duties by – ready for this – "laundering checks." Yes, merely by taking third-party checks from his customers for gold and silver, Sanders became, in the words of one assistant US attorney, "the most dangerous man in the mid-South."

According to Sanders, IRS retired an agent and sent him to work for the Tennessee Department of Revenue with just one goal: indict Sanders for something. At the same time the IRS was cooking up a federal indictment, the ex-IRS agent was brewing one in Tennessee, too.

On 9 January 1990 the IRS descended with SWAT teams on Sanders, his wife, children, and 25 other defendants. However, somewhere along the way, their case went off the tracks. After a trial lasting six months, on 9 July 1991 the Memphis federal jury acquitted all defendants on all charges.

Yet Sanders still had to face Tennessee charges alone. He was indicted under a law that had never been evoked in the 19 years it had stood on the books. He was accused of "delaying and depriving the state of revenue" because he refused to charge sales tax on exchanges of gold and silver money for paper money – you know, like when you give the bank teller a $20 and she hands you back the change, less sales tax. (Oh, they don't do that?)

After a trial in 1993, Sanders was convicted, and eventually spent time in jail. Rather than serve out the onerous conditions of probation – seven years probation with all its costs and 1,000 hours of community service – Sanders went back to jail in 1996 and "flattened out" the sentence (served all of it) to end the whole nightmare.

What Sanders was doing- trying to open a precious metals bank that did not pay sales taxes - might have been entrepreneurial suicide (at least temporarily), but it is part of a larger world view. The topic of the remonetization of silver will be covered below, but Sanders is one of the leading proponents of bringing back silver into everyday economic transactions.[8] Somehow, after Enron, LTCM, the mortgage bubble, and bailouts of banks and corporations without number, Sanders' values, along with those of other silver bugs, don't seem quite so "out there" as they once did.

Robert Kiyosaki and Mike Maloney
goldsilver.com
wealthcycles.com

One of the more successful self-help gurus in the world of investing has been Robert Kiyosaki. You may have been familiar with his "Rich Dad/ Poor Dad" series, which aims to dispel a lot of myths surrounding how one can succeed at growing and maintaining wealth.

Whether or not you think that all of his advice is perfect, or whether or not you agree with everything he has done or said, the unconventional advice put forward by someone like Kiyosaki makes me sit up and take notice. Unconventional advice like: don't be an employee; college isn't for everyone; or that paper cash is trash. A lot of this sounds like the silver story—the idea that you should be very careful drinking too deeply from the well of conventional thought. It is about getting people to break free from group-think, and to investigate alternate ways of thinking, behaving, and living. Of course, Kiyosaki also encourages people to make some money along the way.

Kiyosaki's main precious metals advisor is Michael Maloney, author of the best-selling book on precious metals, *The Rich Dad's Guide to Investing in Precious Metals*. Maloney now runs goldsilver.com, a bullion company based in California, and he offers other educational information through wealthcycles.com. Besides his bullion company, Maloney literally travels the world giving speeches regarding what he terms the "greatest wealth transfer in history," from paper to tangible wealth.

Michael's story also parallels, I think, many of the experiences of the gold and silver bulls. Around the year 2000, Maloney was responsible for finding an asset manager to take care of his widowed mothers' nest egg. The asset manager, following all of the normal asset allocation models, as Maloney relates it, lost nearly half of the money in the account. This kind of drubbing forced Michael- as it has forced many, many others- to consider other ways of looking at investing and speculating. He began to study monetary history, and to understand the damaging impacts of inflation. He also began to seek out the understudied truth that monetary systems and banking systems are often reset once every generation (or so.) These paper systems are far from permanent, and yet gold and silver stand the test of time. At a moment when many are growing concerned about our current monetary system, Maloney understands the potential stampede into physical gold and silver that could still be ahead of us.

The "Crash JP Morgan" Campaign
maxkeiser.com
zerohedge.com
infowars.com

By 2010, the silver story received attention from several other online news entities, many of which may otherwise have little in common with each other. But the scope of the challenges facing western world economies meant that various different groups might need to find common cause in their complaints against elements of our current banking system. Two men in particular, Alex Jones and Max Keiser began to get involved in the "Crash JP Morgan- Buy Silver" campaign. (It still isn't clear to me how this would have worked, but the popularity of the idea spoke to the anger out there regarding precious metals manipulation.) The campaign, for a time, also made it to other alternative investing outlets like zerohedge.com, or kingworldnews.com. Given what I have said about how few people it will take to drive silver prices higher, the fact that several online news outlets were receiving hundreds of thousands and perhaps millions of hits or listeners was wildly bullish for the white metal. It really would only take a few hundred thousand people to try to buy silver in any amount in order for the price to rise exponentially.

In the spring of 2010, many parts of the internet began covering the testimony of Andrew Maguire at a CFTC hearing, where he talked market manipulation in the gold market. This touched off a surge of commentary regarding some of the issues mentioned in this book, particularly about concentrated commercial short positions, as well as how the gold and silver market are susceptible to a bank run, essentially, if holders of paper futures actually tried to get metal. This populist upsurge, which you saw in the U.S. with the Tea Party, or you see in Greece with riots, or elsewhere in Europe or the Middle East, demonstrates that at least for some an increasing distaste for the excesses of big banks (like JP Morgan or Goldman Sachs) is leading many to redefine the nature of their savings and buy tangible assets.

The anger regarding paper manipulation of the metals markets can also be seen in the actions of at least one high-profile billionaire, Eric Sprott, who is helping people put their money where their mouth is by taking delivery of physical silver in protest of abuses in the futures markets.

Eric Sprott
sprott.com

One of the leading hedge fund managers in alternative investing is Eric Sprott. In 1981, Sprott founded Sprott Securities (later Cormark securities) which became one of Canada's largest independently owned securities firms. In 2009, Sprott decided to offer a new gold trust for investors to own in their brokerage accounts, an investment fund that would also pay out physical gold if a shareholder met a certain minimum threshold. In 2010, Sprott further announced that he would be starting a silver trust, where bullion would be stored and fully allocated by the Royal Canadian Mint in Ottawa, Canada. Significantly, the Royal Canadian Mint does not lend out bullion held in its vaults, which is important as Sprott has been critical of the paper games that go on in the precious metals industry. By 2012, Sprott has taken delivery of over 30 million ounces of silver for the PSLV, and intends to take delivery of even more.

In early 2011, Sprott, along with his partner, John Embry, made it clear that they felt the silver market was extremely tight. When they decided to procure several million ounces of silver for their trust, there were several month delays, delays that both men felt were significant. These kinds of delays had not been present with the delivery of gold for their gold fund. When someone who manages billions of dollars makes assertions regarding the tightness in the silver market, you ought to pay attention. This is not someone who is trying to misrepresent market behavior, but someone who became even more alarmed at the tightness in the physical silver market from personal experience.

Sprott has also made it clear that he believes, to varying degrees, that the silver market is manipulated. Of course the term manipulation means different things to different people, but he has asserted that the paper markets are used as a price-capping scheme. He has also been vocal in his critique of the volumes of paper trading, and this played a role in the creation of his silver trust. Through his website and other writings, Sprott warns investors regarding the dangers in the current banking system, and he is an advocate for banking that promotes saving in gold and silver.

For North American investors, the PSLV is likely the only silver-only closed end fund that they can own, even as European investors do have access to the Zurich Cantonal Bank's silver ETF. (The Central Fund of Canada is another closed end precious metals fund, but it invests in both silver and gold.)

Other websites devoted all or part to silver/precious metal investing:

blanchard.com
blog.milesfranklin.com
brotherjohnf.com
caseyresearch.com
chrismartenson.com
dollarcollapse.com
dont-tread-on-me.com
gata.org
gold-eagle.com
goldseek.com
goldmoney.com
harveyorgan.com
jessescrossroadscafe.blogspot.com
jsmineset.com
kereport.com
kingworldnews.com
monex.com
plata.com.mx
sherriequestioningall.blogspot.com
silverdoctors.blogspot.com
silverforecaster.com
silvergoldsilver.com
silverinvestingnews.com
silvermarketnewsonline.com
silversaver.com
silverseek.com
silverstockreport.com
silverstrategies.com
sgtreport.com
tfmetalsreport.com

thevictoryreport.org
zerohedge.com

Chapter 4
A Short History of Silver as Money

In the opening chapter, I mentioned that silver had been "demonetized," meaning that governments no longer hold (significant) stocks of the white metal, and no longer use silver in their currency. Unlike gold, silver isn't even among the reserves held by central banks. But don't let these developments be the last word regarding silver as money. As previously mentioned, silver has every single monetary characteristic inherent to gold: silver is standard in composition, divisible, durable, portable, useful, and cannot be printed. The white metal shares these characteristics with gold in every sense, except that, at present, central banks only hold gold and not silver. However, in earlier eras silver was not simply the money of common people. It was also the money of merchants, bankers, and governments. To some people, silver was just as important as gold as a store of wealth and means of global trade.

Silver, up until about 40 years ago, was arguably the most widely circulated form of metallic money in human history. Along with bronze (which is still in use), it was among the oldest. According to Jonathan Williams, in ancient Mesopotamia and Egypt (roughly 5 thousand years ago), silver by weight functioned as currency (these were not coins, but basically ingots or bars), and legal fines for things like harming another person's property were defined with weights of silver. By the second millennium B.C., the Laws of Eshnunna mandated how much a worker should be paid in silver, and around 700 B.C. in Lydia (present-day Turkey) coins made of electrum (a mixture of gold and silver) came into existence as a means of facilitating trade over long distances. One of the oldest coins in the Middle East, the Hebrew shekel, was a specific weight of silver. For thousands of years, many of the greatest empires in the world used silver coins in their everyday currency (even as they also used copper and gold).[1]

The ancient Greeks used the silver didrachm or tetradrachm (the origin for the modern drachma); the Romans had their silver denarius; the Islamic Caliphate used the dirhem made of silver; and Europeans in the Middle Ages traded with silver sceattas or pennies. The Ottomans of the Near East called their silver coins akces or aspers. In India, people used silver karshapanas until the arrival of the British in the 16th century, when they began using the silver rupee, which would soon become an important coin throughout south Asia.[2]

The Chinese have long possessed a great appreciation for silver, even though their earliest coins were actually copper (before that currency in China was comprised of cowry shells as early as 3000 B.C.). But silver was a far more common store of wealth than gold for Chinese merchants and bankers. It is said that in Chinese the character for bank translates as "silver house," for example. With the discoveries of silver in the New World, the Spanish provided millions of ounces of silver coins to the various Chinese empires after the 16th century. The Spanish Real, or "pieces of eight" was likely the most circulated silver coin in the world, and the coins proved to be quite popular among the Chinese. By the late 19th century, silver became all the more fixed in the Chinese monetary system with the introduction of the Chinese Yuan in 1889. This silver coin was modeled on the widely-used Mexican silver peso (with which it was equally valued). As will be discussed below, the Chinese continued to use millions and millions of ounces of silver until U.S. policies worked to throw the Chinese (along with several other nations) off the silver standard in the 1930s.[3]

Students of Japanese history similarly report that silver coins were far more common than gold coins in those islands, though, as was the case in Southeast Asia, the difficulty in procuring precious metals (at least until the 16th century) meant that many coins in Japan were copper. However, by time of the Meiji in the 1870s, the Japanese created their own silver coinage, the Yen. (This did not last long as the Japanese, as with other western powers, adopted a gold exchange standard by the late 1890s).

If you want to see evidence for the connection between silver and money, look no further than the very word for money in Spanish: the word "plata" means silver, as well as money. In French, one word for money, "argent," is also the word for silver, and the Italian word for money, "denaro" is related to the term for original silver coin of the Roman Empire, the denarius mentioned above. Jerome Smith once claimed that in 51 countries, the word for silver is the same as the word for money.[4] I have not been able to verify this, but it sounds right to me.

So, silver has been used all over the world by millions and millions of people. Silver has also been more than simply the money of the people: in many times and places, silver has been the conduit for transactions between wealthy merchants, states and empires.

Silver Standards

The term "silver standard" may be a foreign one to some readers who understand that in more modern times gold has been the privileged unit of account, used by banks and governments to settle large debts across borders. The rise of central banking- beginning in England in the 1690s- increasingly saw governments and banks favor gold as a way of doing business. This decision also led to wealthy individuals favoring gold over silver, only furthering support for the modern "gold standard."

But before central banks possessed such power in the world, even in Europe, silver could perform not only the role of money within a country, but could also be used to settle debts between countries. Two quotes from England prove the point. In 1698, just before gold was to be favored over silver, a special Report by the Council of Trade stated how it would be impossible "that more than one Metal should be the true Measure of Commerce; and the world by common Consent and Convenience [has] settled that Measure in Silver..."[5] As late as 1730, John Conduitt, director of the English Mint claimed that "an ounce of fine silver is, and always has been, and ought to be, the standing and invariable measure between nation and nation."[6]

Going back to ancient Mesopotamia, in the city of Ur, merchants used silver ingots (not coins) as a means of payment in large transactions (along with wheat and barley); historian Jonathan Williams refers to this as the first "silver standard."[7] In ancient Egypt, it is actually thought that for a time silver was rarer than gold, and it was silver, not gold, that was more commonly thought of as money not only by the people, but also by merchants and others involved in foreign trade. This trend continued into medieval Europe. For example, in Venice in the 13th through 15th centuries, merchants and bankers were just as likely to use silver to settle debts or make large financial transactions, with the use of the above-mentioned denarius, as they were to use gold.[8]

The same was true for medieval merchants in England and in Flanders—gold was not necessarily privileged for the settling of large financial transactions.[9]

At least from the time of the Song Dynasty in China (960-1280), Chinese emperors paid indemnities to foreign powers in silver. One such example was with the state of Liao in 1004, which is an early example of how silver, not gold, was used to settle international debts. Silver continued to play a role in mercantile and banking life in China, especially because of several botched experiments with paper currency.[10] By the late 1400s, irresponsible issuance of paper money led to a near collapse in the Chinese paper money system, and by the 1500s the metallic system returned. The same is true in Persia, where by the 1300s a disastrous experiment in paper money damaged the economy of most of the kingdom, before a hasty return had to be made to honest, metallic money. The Persian silver coins, the dirham, reigned supreme as money throughout the Middle East for nearly 1000 years. (Recently, many Muslims have followed in the footsteps of former Malaysian Prime Minister Dr. Mahathir bin Mohamad in referring to fiat money as evil and not in the spirit of the Koran. They believe that only tangible assets like gold and silver were claimed as money by the founder of their religion.)

Gold/Silver Ratios

History also provides an important perspective into the relative valuation of gold and silver across time and space. Before the active demonetization of silver by the 19th century, the use and popularity of silver with merchants and bankers meant that the price ratio between the two metals was far more narrow than today (meaning that silver's value was greater relative to gold then versus now.) In earlier times, the ratio was as low as 10 ounces of silver for every one ounce of gold, and in some parts of the world (such as Africa and parts of Asia) it was reported that silver was EQUAL to gold in both availability and price.[11] These facts stand in stark contrast to the present, where the ratio of silver to gold has been as high as 80 (or even 100) ounces of silver for every ounce of gold in terms of price.

It is hard to know for certain, but numerous observers at various points in world history observed a ratio of silver to gold of anywhere from 6 to 1 to eight to one. Even after the discovery of massive amounts of silver in the New World beginning in the 1500s moved the ratio towards 15 to 1 in Western Europe, many travelers still observed silver to gold ratios around 10 to 1 in many parts of Africa, the Mid-East, and Asia.

In terms of the relative value of *all* gold bullion to silver, the amount is heavily skewed today in gold's favor, but in the past the exact opposite held true. At several points in history, the total value of all silver bullion was estimated to be worth *more* than the market value of gold. For example, in the mid-1660, there were roughly 1 billion ounces of silver in Europe, while there were only about 30 million ounces of gold. But in pounds sterling, that 1 billion ounces of silver had a cumulative value of roughly 300 million pounds, while the value of all the European gold was only 100 million pounds Sterling.[12] A similar relationship occurred after World War I, where one of the effects of wartime price inflation briefly sent the price of silver to well over one dollar, with the price of gold at twenty dollars. Since there was nearly 30 times more silver coinage in the world than gold, this once again meant that the world's silver held a greater value than all of the gold.[13] Currently, the value of all silver coins and bullion is a fraction (60 billion dollars) of the 3 trillion dollar price tag for all the world's gold. These examples of silver's greater value than gold may simply be a relic from a bygone era, but they may also serve to remind people that silver has played an important part in world monetary history for thousands of years. The fact that it has lost that position over the last 80 years may simply be a temporary phenomenon. Other events or actions from governments or the public may once again restore silver's place as a true monetary metal.

Oftentimes in history the gold/silver ratio implied relative monetary demand for either metal. Today we would talk about "investment demand," meaning where savers want to put their money. As I mentioned above, in the period from 1990 to 2005, the ratio of demand for gold and silver was highly skewed in gold's favor. If you look at what the CPM Group calls "implied net investment" during that period, the ratio of gold to silver purchases was basically infinity to 1 in gold's favor due to investors dumping silver while others were purchasing more gold than they sold. Even as silver coin and bullion is now rarer than gold, this doesn't mean much if investors do not want any silver. But investor apathy towards silver has reversed itself in the last 5 or 6 years, and I think the change could equal a monumental revaluation of the price of silver in the years ahead. During the 1960s and 1970s, investors purchased or hoarded possibly as much as 1.5 to 2 billion ounces of silver before reversing course and selling. As of 2012, investors have likely only purchased at most 500 million ounces after becoming net buyers seven years ago.

Hidden Histories of Debasement

     As I mentioned earlier, debasing money is the oldest trick in the book for governments to get themselves out from under debts that cannot be paid back. This trick is literally thousands of years old. But, as you might expect, don't expect a government official to come out and tell you what they are up to. You have to be smarter than that, and just remember that fiscal belt-tightening or tax increases are often too difficult for any regime or government to implement: so, essentially, governments cheat and just fire up the printing press, or in an earlier time, they mess with the precious metal content of the coinage when debts get out of control.

     Inflation is very much a part of the Silver Story. Just as I said that silver has been used as money in more places and by more people than gold, it is also in the silver coins themselves that we see the process of debasement, or what is usually thought of as inflation. To take the example of the United States, the 40% silver half dollars of 1968 contained far less silver in them than the first American silver half dollar, the Flowing Hair Half Dollar struck in the 1790s. Going back further, when Persia conquered Babylonia in 539 BC many historians estimate that the silver shekel contained sixty percent less silver than the same coin from a couple of centuries before. Among the Greeks, we read in histories of the city states that silver coins were constantly being taken out of circulation and returned with newer issues containing less silver. Debt problems are not new to the Mediterranean region.

     Perhaps the best known case of widespread currency debasement in the ancient world occurred in the later stages of the Roman Empire. For more than 400 years the amount of silver in the denarius fell from 3% all the way down to less than .5% by 275 AD, a decline of over 80%.[14] This debasement is widely seen as the classic result of imperial overreach-- and a warning to many that even the greatest of empires cannot avoid the temptation to cheat savers out of the value of their currency.

Medieval Europeans also lived through numerous debasements of their silver coins over several centuries from 1250 to 1550. In the Ottoman Empire by the 1400s, the Emperor reduced the silver content of his akce silver coins, and tried to penalize anyone trying to sell the older, more valuable silver coins to people who might pay the prevailing, higher market prices further east. As is often the case with government restrictions, the existence of these laws likely indicated illegal smuggling of silver out of the empire (again another way for savers to protect the value of what they have saved.)[15]

Even the most prosperous countries in Europe often succumbed to the temptation of currency debasement. Spain went through it more than once, as the empire began its slow decline after 1600. By the late 1700s, the Spanish peso, or "milled dollar" had been reduced in fineness from roughly 93% to less than 87% silver. Of course, this was done without much fanfare, but it is not a coincidence that this debasement of the Spanish peso paralleled the decline of the once-powerful Iberian state. Although it took longer for the British Empire to decline, the debasement of English sterling coins dated from at least the 1500s.

Another way to debase currency in medieval or early modern times came from the creation of paper money: money that is simply created by the state in whatever amount the state finds convenient to pay off debts to maintain the illusion of solvency. In the 1700s and 1800s, the French endured two very painful experiences with paper money, first in the late 1710s with John Law's scheme, and the second during the French Revolution. After both exercises, paper notes became nearly worthless and governments began to institute laws to try to stop the mad rush being made by the populace into gold and silver.

But many scholars will actually tell you that paper money was first used by the Chinese nearly 1000 years ago. It didn't last, though: hence the greater devotion of the medieval and early modern Chinese to silver. But paper money was seductive to others in Asia. The Monghol Ilkhamid Empire under Geikhatu (1291-1295) tried to reintroduce paper money on the Chinese model by attempting to ban the use of metal currency and force subjects to exchange metal money for the paper note called the ch'ao. The attempt failed with massive inflation and economic stagnation, and the following emperor, Ghazan, needed to mint a silver coin in order to restore confidence in the monetary system.[16]

Even during the days when governments were supposed to be on a gold standard (meaning their currency to some extent was convertible into gold), it was still possible for governments to go off the gold standard. This amounted to devaluation. For example, Great Britain went off the gold standard during the Napoleonic Wars, its debt skyrocketed, and there was a severe shortage of silver and gold coins. This would eventually lead to the Great Recoinage of 1816, which aided Britain in maintaining a stable currency for nearly a hundred years. And yet by 1914, Britain was forced again to go off the gold standard due to the need for deficit spending to fight World War I.[17]

If possible, governments will do what they can to hide the fact that they are debasing people's savings. You have to admit that this makes sense from the perspective of a government trying to get away with the sleight of hand of stealing from savers.

Silver and the Rise of the West

Europeans have, over the last several centuries, played the dominant role in increasing the production of silver, either through new technologies or mine discoveries. For many centuries, silver stimulated world trade and bought many luxury items for western Europeans, in turn aiding numerous transformations in European society, ranging from urbanization, to the slave trade, to industrialization. It is worth looking back at this part of the silver story.

In medieval Europe, silver at times could be quite scarce, along with gold. But slowly, by 1300, new mines in central Europe, from Bohemia to Serbia enabled Europeans to begin to increase their silver output to nearly 1 million ounces a year.[18] But this increase in supply still was not enough to finance trade, or to meet monetary demand for metal. By the early 1400s, historians say that Europe was once again suffering from a lack of silver. It was at this point, that Europeans established breakthroughs in mining that enabled them to increase output. By 1460, merchants and engineers helped to develop new water pump technologies to re-open flooded older mines. In addition, the liquation process is believed to have been discovered around this time, or at least made more practical in its use. Liquation is a way of separating out copper from silver by heating the silvery copper with lead. The copper essentially attaches to the lead and the silver coalesces on its own. The liquation technology would be the primary means of separating silver from lead or copper until the nineteenth century when miners discovered more efficient methods.

In the aftermath of these new discoveries in mine technology, dramatic increases in mine output came from newer mines in Saxony (near historic mines at Freiberg and in Bohemia), in addition to new mines in what is now southern Austria. Such discoveries enabled mine production to once again move above the one million ounce a year mark by 1480, and it would only increase in the years ahead. Increased silver production allowed Europe to pay for much-coveted spices, silks, or other luxury items from the Middle East and Asia. Much of this trade centered in Venice, since the merchants there were best positioned to take advantage of the Eastern trade. By 1500, nearly 500,000 ounces of silver left Venice to purchase goods from the East. This dynamic-- European silver leaving the continent on its way east-- would continue for several centuries.

The ability of Europeans to buy more and more things with silver also increased dramatically with their conquest of the Americas. In the 1500s, Europeans stumbled upon the greatest silver discovery in modern human history when the Spanish invaded Mexico and Peru. This conquest also dramatically increased mine production, or more accurately, greatly accelerated an already upward moving trend in mine supply. By 1600, silver mine supply briefly hit 15 million ounces, roughly a fifteen fold increase from 1450. (However production would settle down toward 12 million ounces by 1700, not to surpass 15 million ounces again until the 1740s).[19]

With the help of Native Americans (whom they often worked to death), the Spanish began to drain the New World of millions of ounces a year of silver. After roughly 1530, silver began flowing from Mexico to Europe and beyond. However it was not until the 1540s that the great silver discoveries in Potosi, Bolivia, and Zacatecas, San Luis Potosi, and Guanajuato in Mexico occurred. The mines in Potosi were infamous for their use of the mercury amalgamation process, since there was a steady supply of mercury from nearby Peru. This amalgamation process proved effective at releasing silver from lower grade deposits, but, obviously, the use of mercury had poisonous and tragic impacts on the native miners used to do the labor.

Bolivia and Peru would soon provide two-thirds of Spanish silver production. All of this new American silver meant that Spain would play a greater role in the western silver market. By 1600, the Dutch (under Spanish influence) formed the United Dutch East India Company and Amsterdam replaced Venice as the main hub for the financing and trading in silver bullion.[20] The Dutch would also play a large role in shipping silver from Japan, which went through a miniature boom in silver mining as well in the 1600s.

Over the course of the 1600s, there was a drop off in global silver production from a high of 15 million ounces, down to around 12 million ounces, but most silver still came from the New World (Peru, Bolivia, Mexico) via Spain. However, by 1640, London began to play a greater role in this silver trade. As the English began to play a larger role in New World colonization (and therefore became a stronger European power) more and more of the silver trade moved from Amsterdam to London (even as London would not finally surpass Amsterdam until the late 1700s). Significantly, Moses Mocatta moved to London in the 1670s, establishing a trading house that would later become Scottia-

Mocatta. For many years, Scottia-Mocatta dominated the silver price fixing. When in 1717 an unidentified buyer tried to corner the silver market through a purchase of over a million ounces of silver (just under 9% of all global production), they went through Mocatta. When the corner failed, Mocatta worked with the Bank of England to unwind the position, thus cementing Mocatta's relationship with the Bank of England.[21]

The Accidental Gold Standard?

For many years, populists or other critics of the monopoly power of central banks took a very critical view of the gold standard, which is something to be addressed below. These critics felt that the gold standard was established on purpose to subvert the ability of the free market to conduct trade. The move away from a free market, bimetallic monetary standard symbolized the dramatic concentration of power being made by a system of central bankers, and the banishment of silver from the monetary system (in many respects) only furthered populist anger against new, modern forms of financial power. Although there is evidence that the creation of the gold standard was in some sense accidental, not everyone agrees with this version of history.

It is true that gold, across time and space, has been rarer than silver. But the view of gold as an unrivaled unit of account has a history: a history that begins in the 18th century. Oddly enough, silver came under pressure in Europe as a unit of account precisely because silver was in such high demand in Asia.

In 1717, the constant drain of silver away from England received the notice of both the king as well as of the Master of the English mint, Sir Isaac Newton. Newton undertook the first systematic analysis of the relative market valuation of gold to silver. He came to the conclusion that the English Crown was mispricing silver in its official mandate for the value of its currency. Newton recommended the king decrease the official price of gold to one pound five pence, but this markdown still was not enough to prevent the drain of silver out of the kingdom. Gold remained overvalued at the mint where it was taken in for coinage. Britain was basically on a gold standard, since so much silver left England, and over the course of the 1700s only 5 million ounces of silver was coined in the country. The guinea was based on gold, not silver.[22]

Over the course of the next century and a half, the rise of England and her central bank meant that gold would play an ever greater role in international finance. The International Gold Standard was more or less in place by the 1840s, meaning that the western world pegged its currencies to the price of gold in an effort to create exchange rate stability.

However, it is important to remember that when people talk about a "gold standard" for international banks and governments, they are actually talking about something that was quite recent, and that did not last that long (roughly 1800 to 1914, depending upon how you define terms.)

Silver As A Crisis Hedge

The idea of silver as a crisis hedge, then, was dealt several blows in the nineteenth and twentieth centuries, particularly between roughly 1867 and 1934. In these years, silver was not really the go-to asset during severe banking panics, and its price consistently dropped due to the double whammy of concerted demonetization from governments as well as huge increases in mine supply.

But if we focus on the period before 1867, we find that market silver prices- like gold- achieved significant premiums to their fixed prices during times of severe economic and political stress. Of course, it was sometimes difficult for average people to realize this profit, since the silver would have to either be exported out of the country, or, more likely realized by selling it to someone desperate enough to pay you more than the fixed amount. At any rate, both in Britain and the United States, according to Ray Jastram, there were several moments when the market price of silver spiked higher than the official rate. During the period of the American Revolutionary War (1775-83) as well as during the Napoleonic Wars, the market price of silver reached as high as 30 pence an ounce, which was about 18% higher than the fixed price of just under 26 pence.[23] In the United States, during the War of 1812 a larger than 10% premium was realized on a silver ounce, when the market price went over 1.43, even as the official price was 1.28.

In these cases, due either to the shocks of war or severe financial depression, the convertibility of bank notes into gold or silver was normally suspended, and yet some merchants or others would continue to trade in the metals to try to realize a profit off of other's panic. During the American Civil War, the market price of silver reached a high it would not achieve again until over a century later: in 1864 the market price hit 2.55 an ounce, for a premium of over 80%.[24] That was an amazing high for silver, considering how eighty years later, the market price of silver would drop to below 30 cents. But the overall point is that even under a metallic standard of some sort, you have periods of financial crisis and people will bid the metals up in a scramble for real money.

These periods of depression or of a suspension of convertibility are also a reminder that even under a fixed metallic standard, governments don't maintain a perfect record of managing their budgets or of preventing banking panics. Some things don't change, no matter what the monetary standard. What has changed in more recent times is the ability of average people to take part in a silver "market." Remember that traditionally it just was not that easy to buy and sell the precious metals—there were few exchanges devoted to this trade, and normally governments and mints tried to discourage what they would have termed "arbitrage" (meaning the ability to take advantage of mispriced assets between countries or even within them.) In many other times and places, ownership of gold or silver bullion have been criminalized.

Part of the silver story today is how our current markets allows for so many people to take advantage of owning silver, not only through online bullion dealerships and storage, but also through a bevy of new silver exchange trade funds and closed-end funds. You are really only a mouse click from being able to take part in the silver story.

Silver Demonetization- The Crimes of 1867 and 1873

Many developments in the 1800s damaged the reputation of silver as a monetary metal. In fact, there are at least five reasons why silver was slowly banished from the international monetary system (even as it was still used in common coinage). First off, the voracious demand for silver in India (and a lesser extent China) continued to make the price unstable, or more accurately, it was difficult to control

107

silver flows. If eastern demand grew, there could be silver shortages in Europe, but conversely, if silver mine supply grew at the same time as silver demand weakened in the east, the silver price could plummet. So the wide-spread belief that silver was somehow unreliable further encouraged Britain to begin to privilege gold over silver with its bank notes, and as the British Empire grew after 1815, other European nations also decided to keep up with the leader in terms of gold. As mentioned above, this development occurred in conjunction with the rise of central banking. To only sweeten the pot for gold standard supporters, new gold mine discoveries in California, Australia, and, later, Alaska ensured that there would be enough gold to back bank notes or other forms of debt. Additionally, silver mine production began to surge in a way it had not done before or since, and this only furthered the idea that silver really wasn't "hard money."

Then came the decision of Germany to try to emulate Britain in terms of a gold standard. By 1873, Germans began to liquidate their silver holdings in exchange for gold. Unfortunately, the French also decided to curtail silver purchases, some would say in an effort to damage the Germans' effort to increase gold in their monetary system through silver sales. This monetary war could not have come at a worse time. The flood of new silver from the Comstock Load in Nevada (discovered in 1859) in addition to a drop off in Indian demand worked to collapse the market price of silver by roughly 25% over the course of the late 1800s. This downdraft in the silver market only encouraged other nations to limit the production of silver to small coins. The trauma being experienced in the silver market also threated to damage the entire monetary system because of the practice of too rigid monetary ratios at the mint.[25]

You have to remember that when government mints maintained fixed ratios, they could not, or would not, easily adapt their official ratio to market movements. Most mints had maintained a gold to silver ratio of 1 ounce of gold to every 15 or 16 ounces of silver. But as the price of silver dropped, speculators could buy silver 40 or 50% less than face value, bring the silver into mints that would accept the metal and realize a profit (for example if the market price for a silver ounce was 40 cents, but the mint recognized its value at 1 dollar, you have your bullion made into coins at the mint and more than double your money.)

By 1873, led by France, but soon to be followed by the U.S., silver was eliminated from large parts of the international monetary system. Even India, for a period of time in 1893, closed their mints to silver. From then on, the Bank of England, or other central banks, would honor the idea that loans or credits given between central banks could be convertible into gold. If gold stock was flowing away from a country, interest rates would have to rise, and the domestic economy had to be suppressed to curtail imports. This rigidity of course was resented by many, most of all poorer people and workers. But the period from 1815 to 1915 was a period of great prosperity and peace, at least in Western Europe, and many have seen the British-led gold standard as at least part of the reason behind this prosperity.[26]

Silver as the "People's Metal"

As mentioned earlier, the Gold Standard was hardly loved or appreciated by rural, western, or poorer Americans far away from the power centers of London, Paris, or Berlin. Many average people felt that a state-mandated, monometallic standard hindered the free market.

By the late 1800s, historians talk about a broad movement with the name "Populists" that advocated relief against the deflation in farm prices, and that also complained about the vast concentrations of wealth arising from the "monied power." Remember that the late 1800s was the beginning of a transition in the U.S. from a rural nation to an industrial one, but that transition left many average people behind. Many of the complaints made by Populists should be familiar to you today: complaints about needless financial speculation on Wall Street, anger over monopolistic practices by railroads or other well-connected corporations, and disgust that the political system was easily bought off by special interests. Many of the populists believed that the free coinage of silver was a solution, or at least something that westerners deserved in their battle to fight against depressed prices. Other populists wanted to go further, and hoped that the government could somehow better regulate this new and scary capitalist system.

If you are reading this as an advocate of "hard money," you can understand why the "silverites" or populists were not popular with many businessmen or with creditors. Businessmen feared that the populists were simply trying to forcibly redistribute wealth, or create regulations that would hamper business investment. Creditors saw in the free coinage of silver simply a way to inflate away debts, since to coin more silver would mean to increase the money supply. Wealthier Americans were shocked that Bryan would so openly criticize the gold standard, a standard which to them seemed to be a source of international monetary stability.

The Populist movement found support from enough members of the Democratic Party to put forth William Jennings Bryan as a Presidential candidate in 1896. Bryan ran on a platform of widespread reform: he not only wanted the free coinage of silver, but also government aid to farmers and others among the down and out. (Bryan, I might add, later on became a supporter of the Federal Reserve, since he hoped that somehow the banking system could be regulated for the benefit of the people….) But Bryan lost the election, and the silver issue went away, at least for a while.

To take the large picture view of the late 1800s, silver was pitted against gold- one metal, gold, seemed to stand for monetary sanity, conservatism, and austerity- the other metal, silver, seemed to represent a newer and dangerous desire to expand the money supply and release limitless amounts of credit into the financial system. Of course, in many ways, the simple fact that silver mining exploded in the late 1800s also did silver in as a hard currency. And as I've argued throughout this book, silver still has not recovered from the days when it seemed to many to be nothing more than an easily extractable, cheap, and plentiful metal sought after by debtors as a means of cheating their economic betters.[27]

Silver, the Federal Reserve, and the Pittman Act

However, elements of the inflation-friendly agenda of the Populists later found support under more respectable Progressives like President Woodrow Wilson, who included William Jennings Bryan in his cabinet in 1913. In fact, you could say that those who supported silver so strongly in the 1890s were (in some cases inadvertently) laying the foundations for an economic system, under the Federal Reserve, that supported inflation, or easy credit. Murray Rothbard, among other economists, criticized the Federal Reserve for purposefully pursuing a policy of inflating the money supply, a policy that coincided with the decline of the gold standard outlined above. Such pro-inflation policies were also being pursued by the federal government: one example can be seen with the Pittman Act of 1918. This act increased the amount of silver that the Treasury had to buy from domestic silver miners at a price of 1 dollar- which was nearly double the market rate for the metal. This was a way of expanding the base money supply, or the amount of currency in circulation, since silver was still used in small transactions at the time. In conjunction with this act of Congress, a leading member of the Federal Reserve in the early 1920s, Benjamin Strong has been accused by several monetary historians of colluding with Montagu Norman, of the Bank of England, to keep American interest rates artificially low as a way of allowing the British Pound to remain artificially strong. In February 1922, Norman hailed the easy credit in America and urged further decreases in interest rates.

The other economic problem confronting the world of the 1920s had to do with a badly damaged economic system after the waste and carnage of World War I. Policy elites were trying to manage the situation, believing that they could avoid further calamities caused by overextended governments bankrupted by war. Of course the central planners proved unsuccessful at these efforts, and the Crash of 1929 occurred on the watch of the very institution, the Federal Reserve, which was founded to supposedly stop these kinds of catastrophes. Many then and now blamed loose money policies- often using silver as a conduit for inflation- as a prime cause for the unsustainable boom and bust of the late 1920s and early 1930s.[28] But the leaders of the western financial system had become addicted to inflation, and continued to pursue policies leading to weak paper currencies in the years ahead.

The Silver Purchase Act of 1934 and More Demonetization

The demand for credit expansion made by those who wanted more inflation only made a stronger and more determined return after the Crash of 1929. In the United States, the election of Franklin D. Roosevelt signaled a turn toward more government intervention in the market to prop up the credit system. The actions of the Roosevelt administration also demonstrated that the emerging Dollar Reserve system would be based on inflation to its core. Roosevelt and his advisors made this clear in depths of the Great Depression. Among other things, these American leaders focused on two policies: one was to devalue the dollar versus gold, and the other was to begin a silver buying program to prop up the price of silver on global markets (and therefore create inflation).

Roosevelt's gold policy was part of a larger attempt made by many western powers to stoke the fires of inflation to get the credit system moving again. Executive Order 6102, passed in 1933, also claimed to confiscate gold bullion (people were asked to turn in their gold), though in fairness there were few prosecutions for people holding onto their gold. Roosevelt's silver purchase program, initiated in 1934, did nationalize silver stocks, as well as curtail speculation in silver. In fact the act mandated that the young COMEX exchange turn over its stock of silver to the government and forbade futures trading in the metal. Roosevelt and his supporters also pushed through the Silver Transfer Tax which was a 50% tax on domestic silver transactions. This law aimed to stop speculators from benefitting from the intentions of the U.S. Treasury to raise the price of silver.[29] But senators from silver producing regions like Montana, Colorado, or Nevada felt their regions deserved this special treatment, and many were still bitter over the legacies of the Crimes of 1867 and 1873, where silver had been demonetized.

The decision made by the U.S. government to prop up the price of silver meant that silver was pouring into the United States. This was setting the stage for American dominance in both gold stockpiles and silver stockpiles. As usual however, there were several unintended consequences of the silver purchase program. Roosevelt, in trying to get inflation going within the United States did not apparently care that if he increased the price of silver too much, he could cause monetary chaos with countries still on a silver standard- such as Mexico, Peru, or China. A rising silver price would be deflationary to those countries, and these states would have to scramble to institute a new paper money regime. According to Roy Jastram, China was thrown into a serious deflationary spiral in the mid-1930s. By 1935, China was furious with the Roosevelt administration, and ordered a nationalization of silver in exchange for paper notes. The Silver Purchase Program also badly damaged the status of silver as a monetary metal in many parts of the world, from Spain, to Siam, to Japan, and Mexico.[30]

World currencies had been threatened by heavy handed American policies, and yet some will argue that by pushing countries to debase currencies or go to paper outright, Roosevelt was setting the stage for a modern monetary order much more lenient and accepting of rising debt levels and inflation. When you look back at the way the U.S. Federal Reserve and Congress have so often pursued policies of currency debasement (the dollar has lost something like 98% of its purchasing power since 1913) it is not surprising that the rise of the Dollar Reserve standard, made official by 1945, is so intertwined with a love of inflation and debt.

Silver's First Industrial Revolution and Mining Transformations

The demonetization of silver also occurred at a time when silver supplies grew enormously. Monetary historian Pierre Vilar once estimated that global silver mine production rose from around 40 million ounces a year in 1850 to over 160 million ounces a year by 1900.[31] The late 19th century growth rate in silver production has not been repeated since. Such huge increases in silver mine production only furthered the impression that silver wasn't that rare, wasn't that special, and wasn't really a monetary metal.

The transformations in the mining of silver greatly aided in this increased mine supply. The liquation and mercury amalgamation processes for extracting silver from low grade ores were being surpassed by newer technologies, such as the Parkes Process, discovered by Alexander Parkes in 1850. Parkes found a way to add zinc to the silver and lead ores that could enable the extraction of silver. Meanwhile, by the 1860s miners were experimenting with new technologies for extracting ores from the ground itself. The discovery of the Comstock lode in Nevada, also encouraged greater experimentation with new steam and hydraulic systems. Different kinds of power drills and explosives all aided in the success of various mines associated with the Virginia City mining district to dig deeper and better manage the possibility of flooding (an ever-present risk with any form of mining). Bulk mining also became more prevalent in North America by 1900, one of many new underground mine techniques to more effectively dig out hard to reach material. In the early 1900s, newer electro-refining techniques further enabled miners to extract more silver from base metal production (such as zinc, lead or copper). In fact the explosion of base metal production itself in the late 19th and early 20th centuries also meant that silver production would similarly increase.

You could really say that the period from 1870 to 1930 saw silver dethroned as a precious metal in the mind of some. During the Great Depression in the United States, silver output was 5 TIMES greater than demand---this one fact reveals just how plentiful silver had become by the early 20th century.[32]

The cultural legacy of the idea of cheap, industrial silver, in my opinion, is one of many image problems facing silver. It was not that long ago that people conceived of silver as practically a base metal, not in the same league as gold. But quietly, as I have argued elsewhere, silver supplies dwindled and the metal is now rarer than gold in monetary form. And yet, few seem to know or care. At least for now.

Changing Centers for the Silver Market

At some point in the mid-20th century, the United States became the focus for the world silver market. Perhaps unsurprising news, when you think about it, given the fact that the U.S. was a major creditor nation to Europe, and the country soaked up all sorts of silver because of the Silver Purchase Act. The United States soon became the world's center for commodity and stock speculation. Although silver trading was illegal in the United States until the 1960s, the huge stockpile possessed by the government would ensure the centrality of New York as the center of the world silver market, as well. At one point, it is estimated that the silver possessed by the US approached 5 billion ounces. However, today, the United States only has something around 30-50 million ounces of silver, and the same roughly holds true for the COMEX (excluding inventories deposited there for private clients.) Apart from possessing the world's reserve currency (the dollar) there really isn't any major reason for the silver price to still be set in New York (more on this below.) But the dominance of the COMEX division of the New York mercantile exchange speaks to the legacy of what was once the greatest silver hoard in the world.

The Final Demonetization

Although the Silver Purchase Act of 1934 damaged the status of silver as a monetary metal by forcing countries to debase or turn to paper money, several western nations like the U.S., Great Britain, and Germany did continue to coin silver- in the case of Germany until 1974. In the United States, the last coins in circulation with any silver content were made in 1968. This final push to demonetize silver came in conjunction with American leaders wanting a purely fiat dollar, in addition to a strong industrial demand finally outstripping supplies.

For the two decades before 1960, global industrial demand for silver had been anywhere from 150 million to as high as 230 million ounces a year. Over the course of the 1960s, industrial demand then grew from 239 million all the way up to near 400 million ounces a year; it would peak at over 430 million ounces in 1973. By the 1960s, then, pressures were mounting on the US Treasury to maintain the

117

silver content of its coinage. The US Treasury ceased sales of silver to industrial users, but it was clear to President Kennedy that the silver content of US currency would have to go. Kennedy then fully repealed the Silver Purchase Act of 1934, and also eliminated silver backing for one and two dollar silver certificates. Treasury stocks of silver continued to decline, with over 500 million ounces of sales between 1964 and 1967 alone. 1964 was the last year of the 90% silver coinage (dimes, quarters, half-dollars), though a reduced silver content "clad" half-dollar would continue in circulation until 1968.[33]

Another important development in 1963 was the reopening of silver futures contracts at the COMEX, since restrictions on owning silver bullion ended with the repeal of the Silver Purchase Act. With the reopening of the market, trading in silver futures at New York was fairly small: a mere 40 million ounces traded during the entire year of 1963.[34] But slowly, more and more participants became accustomed to the use of purely paper contracts (and leverage) to buy and sell silver futures. Around 1969 as well, several brokerages, led by the Pacific Coast Coin Exchange (later known as Monex) allowed retail investors to buy silver on margin. With the end of official government sales, and now that silver had been completely taken out of the currency, people could speculate on the silver price.[35] Presumably a futures market would also be a place where producers and users might be able to hedge prices (essentially taking out insurance against prices going up or down). But as with the history of commodity futures, the speculative, gambling element to silver became irresistible to many. Within a couple of years, this desire for speculation would see the greatest "long" concentration of all time in the silver market with the arrival of Bunker and Herbert Hunt.

The Importance of 1971

Anyone remotely familiar with precious metals investing knows that in August of 1971, President Richard Nixon removed any and all gold backing to the U.S. dollar, the reserve currency of the world. This final act was simply the last in a long line of decisions made in the post 1945 world to diminish the importance of gold in the international financial system.

But the final act made by Nixon against gold galvanized various different groups of people to encourage greater ownership of the precious metals. James U. Blanchard, III was one of the better known leaders of the movement to legalize gold bullion ownership in the United States. He founded the National Committee to Legalize Gold (NCLG) in 1971. Blanchard famously arranged for a biplane to tow a "Legalize Gold" banner over President Nixon's 1973 inauguration, and Blanchard organized press conferences where he would show off gold bars that at the time were currently illegal for Americans to own. The efforts of Blanchard and others paid off in 1974, when President Gerald Ford signed a bill authorizing the private ownership of gold. In the 1970s, hundreds of new gold bullion dealers came into existence, at least in the United States. This was a huge support to the bull market in gold and silver in the 1970s.[36]

The other big support for gold and silver prices came from the efforts of the Texas billionaires, Nelson Bunker and William Herbert Hunt to essentially remonetize silver. According to most accounts, Nelson Bunker Hunt's interest in silver was sparked by a conversation with commodity trader, Alvin J. Brodsky. Brodsky appealed to Hunt's concern over inflation, as well as over the diminished power of American might in the world epitomized by U.S. military failures in Vietnam. Hunt was no normal billionaire. He was someone who possessed strong views regarding the decline of morals in the United States, was a staunch anti-Communist and member of the John Birch Society. He also possessed a personal distaste for the rising power of Arab leaders like Muammar Quadaffi. There was good reason for Hunt to hate the Libyan leader: Quadaffi had been making it difficult for the Texas oilman to profit on one of his biggest oil discoveries in Libya. Many have said that other silver bugs, such as Dallas commodity dealers Don and Scott Dial, as well as the successful author, Jerome Smith only further encouraged Hunt in his efforts to own silver. Since it was technically illegal for Americans to own gold bullion, silver seemed to be the next best thing to buy as a dollar hedge.

Initially, Hunt purchased less than 100,000 ounces of silver, with the help of Brodsky, who worked at the commodity trading firm, Bache, Halsey, Stuart, and Shields. But these purchases helped to push the silver price up to three dollars an ounce by 1973. And other events only increased Bunker Hunt's desire to fight back against an economic system he saw as working against him. For one, Quadaffi went forward that year with plans to nationalize Hunt's oil holding in Libya, and the Justice Department opened up an investigation into Bunker's wiretapping of an employee accused by Hunt of embezzling funds. (This investigation soon led to an indictment for obstruction of justice). It was late in 1973 that word began to spread of the Hunts trying to lead a corner in the silver market. By 1974, the brothers had amassed futures contracts equaling over 50 million ounces of silver, or roughly 10 percent of global supply. More importantly, the Hunts took delivery of all of their silver, unlike most futures traders, who simply rolled over paper contracts. The Hunts even went through the trouble of personally flying their silver to safety in Switzerland.

Not long after taking delivery of his silver, Hunt went to the floor of the New York exchange, where trading stopped as people got to observe the overweight, spectacled Texan trying to corner the silver market. Hunt also delivered a rare interview where he laid out now familiar arguments about the need to hold tangible assets: "Just about anything you buy, rather than paper, is better." Hunt then quipped, "any damn fool can run a printing press."[37]

But if Hunt were going to be able to keep his corner going (and get the price of silver to rise further), he needed more help. By 1975, Hunt was a bit cash squeezed due to legal disputes over his father's estate, in addition to other expensive business ventures. So Bunker headed to the Middle East in March of 1975, and first tried to get the Iranian royal family to help him in his efforts to buy more silver. The Iranians gave no firm commitment, so Bunker decided to try the Saudis. However, the assassination of King Faisal put a halt to those plans. And so Bunker's silver investment languished with the market in 1975 (even though the price had started to perk up after the 1974 recession). Hunt would branch out to other mining and commodity investments, including an ultimately unsuccessful bid to own the nation's largest silver mine, held by the Sunshine Mining Company.

The silver price began to move higher again by 1977 partly due to renewed interest from investors in gold bullion. According to Timothy Green, there was also an emerging, strong long side bias even among many financial institutions in gold futures at this time, something that may come as a surprise to current readers more accustomed to large commercial traders being perennially short precious metals.[38] But gold, like silver, was gaining a following as the dollar continued to move lower in the late 1970s.

The Hunts continued to work on creating a vehicle to get others involved in owning silver bullion. The creation of International Metals Investment Company in 1979 with assistance from Saudi businessmen Sheik Aboud Al-Amoudi and Sheik Bin Mussalem, represented an attempt by the Hunts to take delivery of 90 million ounces of silver. The Hunts needed to come up with 450 million dollars to do this.

This is where large banks such as Continental Illinois Bank, the Royal Bank of Canada, First National Bank of Chicago, and the New York branch of Swiss Bank extended the Hunts nearly 200 million dollars in loans. Many reports later stated that these loans were done directly against the wishes of then Federal Reserve chairman Paul Volker, who did not want banks to make loans for commodity speculation.

But the loans were made in any event, and by the fall of 1979, the Hunt- Saudi partnership took delivery of 40 million of the 90 million ounces they desired to physically own. They also managed to get another 28 million ounces held outside the COMEX vaults. In response to these actions, the CFTC contacted the Hunts about their concentrated position, but did not take action. However, the Chicago Board of Trade (another exchange where the Hunt's held positions) did decide to take action, declaring that no trader could have more than 3 million ounces of futures contracts.

For his part, Bunker felt that this was another conspiracy of eastern elites against him. To some extent he was correct: later it was widely reported that several exchange members both in Chicago and New York held short positions in silver approaching 2 billion dollars.

Meanwhile, as 1980 approached, the price of silver continued to rocket higher and higher, rising to over 25 dollars an ounce. At this point, the CFTC reversed its earlier view and decided to endorse the COMEX in its move against the Hunt led silver consortium. In January, the COMEX announced that no trader could have more than 10 million ounces of futures contracts: the Hunts currently had 90 million. The Hunts did not think this was a problem, since they continued to buy on the European market. But then the COMEX took even more drastic action against all long silver speculators: the exchange would stop allowing long contracts! However, trading was still open in Chicago and elsewhere in Europe, and the price did not immediately drop.

Prices did begin to drop in response to several other factors, however. One, people began dumping all kinds of silverware and jewelry on the market, with such high silver prices. Two, the high prices were discouraging more speculative interest (no doubt helped along by the COMEX restrictions). But finally, Paul Volker was dramatically hiking interest rates in a move to rein in inflation. According to some, Volker was also taking aim at commodity speculators, and events moved quickly. By March 25, 1980, the Hunts owed over 130 million dollars to their broker, Bache. Bunker's brother, Herbert, informed Bache that they could not make the payment. This was a major problem, and meant the firm might lose over 30 million dollars and possibly go out of business. Financial leaders including Paul Volker closely watched the silver market. In response to this, though, Bunker Hunt began talking about some sort of silver-backed bond, in an apparent effort to try to rekindle investor interest in silver.

Then came "Silver Thursday," March 27, 1980, where a near thirty percent decline in silver in one day (from

16 dollars to 11 dollars) sent shockwaves through the stock market. Compared to where silver had been just a few weeks earlier (from between 30 dollars to nearly 50) some traders lost from 50-70% on their investments in a matter of weeks. In the press, many began to make comparisons to the Great Depression, even though the damage was largely contained to the commodity markets. In the following weeks and months the Hunts needed to negotiate with their lenders, including the Engelhard association, and the brothers then needed to turn to Paul Volker to help work out some sort of loan package to see the brothers through. With the help of banks such as the First National of Dallas and Morgan Guaranty of New York, the Hunts were able to slowly pay off creditors. The Hunts later filed for bankruptcy, since the price of silver continued to plummet in the 1980s.

At their peak, the Hunts concentrated long position of over 90 million ounces at the COMEX equaled over 25% of global mine production, although it accounted for less than 5% of known bullion stockpiles at the time. In terms of price, the value of the world's silver briefly equaled the monetary base of the United States (in present-day terms this would put silver somewhere close to 2000 dollars an ounce, give or take). Earlier in 1980, when gold peaked, the value of gold EXCEEDED the market capitalization of the US stock market by roughly 15%, which today would put gold at over 15,000 dollars an ounce![39]

This whole episode involving the Hunts and the COMEX exchange burned many investors, and was not popular with the then-Federal Reserve chief Paul Volker. For these reasons, we have to yet to see a similar long side concentration in silver. But if we did, you could certainly expect the price to rocket far higher and faster than it has in the last decade. Remember, the price rise in silver since 2001 has occurred against the backdrop of a persistent (if slowly declining) concentrated short position at the COMEX. There has yet to be a real short squeeze in silver, and there has yet to be another long side silver concentration like the Hunts.[40]

Government Price Suppression

The fact that Treasury Secretary Paul Volker was none too pleased about the amount of money banks and brokerages were pouring into the silver market in 1980 also underscores an important point concerning the role of the government in trying to influence the price of hard assets, even as they have allowed for private individuals to own and trade them. As you might imagine, governments and their central banks try to use asset prices to guide policies, or to otherwise use the bully pulpit of financial repression to get unsuspecting savers to stay in "government favored" assets.

If you go to the website of the Gold Anti-Trust Action Committee, gata.org, you will find several documented statements made by men like Paul Volker or Alan Greenspan concerning their desire not to see the prices of tangible assets (especially gold) rise in a disorderly fashion. In a world where central banks try to purposefully weaken or strengthen their national currencies, and in a world where savers are told to move their money back into the stock market or else (the purpose of zero percent interest rates) it should come as little surprise that those who think they can shape and mold public opinion want to try to influence prices for assets traded on world markets. The problem is, not all world leaders think the same way regarding a given asset's price (compare China's more positive official view on precious metals versus the more negative view in the U.S.), nor do central planners possess unlimited power to control the average person in their financial decisions.

Other Billionaires and Silver

So just because the government may not like private efforts to drive up the price of hard assets like silver, this does not mean that the super-rich have ignored the white metal. Although he has recently made negative comments on gold, Warren Buffet (along with Bill Gates) did own quite a lot of silver at one time. Beginning in 1997, Buffett began acquiring what became a 130 million ounce investment in silver. The reasoning for his purchase at the time was due to the silver deficit then prevailing in the marketplace. Hundreds of millions of ounces of silver were being consumed because of insufficient mine supply, and yet the metal's price had actually been dropping over the course of the 1990s. Buffett and Berkshire Hathaway maintained that this situation could not continue forever. Interestingly, at the time, according to several articles, a lawsuit was actually filed accusing Buffett of manipulation. However, Buffett was able to acquire the 130 million ounces, which meant that he at one time owned more silver than the COMEX exchange. Less than ten years later, Buffett sold his silver position, making a profit, but a small one. Many believe his initial investment at around 5.50 dollars an ounce only increased at most 40 percent to about 7.50 an ounce by the time the sales were complete in 2006. Still, many wondered why he sold too soon, and while he would not give specific answers, Buffett admitted that he "bought silver early and sold it early...speculation is wildest at the end."[41]

The Buffet purchase though, was met with a certain degree of skepticism and disbelief by the broader silver market. According to the CPM Group, the physical silver market actually responded to Buffett's purchases by ramping up sales. Many burned silver holders wanted out and they got their chance with Buffett. This may also have dampened the impact of Buffett's purchase on the price of silver bullion, and certainly indicates the deep skepticism among many in the late 1990s that silver would ever be much of a good investment (or that it would ever increase much above 6 or 7 dollars an ounce). You want to contrast this point to the present, where retail investors are now acquiring silver—not selling it.

Buffett likely sold out from his silver position because he saw that the silver deficit situation was coming to an end. Buffett mainly felt that silver was worth owning as a speculation on industrial demand, not as an investment in a safe-haven or because silver has been money for thousands of years. While he did not say so publicly, other commentators also pointed out that Buffett did not want to be accused of trying to corner the silver market, like the Hunts some twenty five years earlier. This also may have influenced his decision to sell his large position, even though the position was not largely on paper, but was in fact actual metal (unlike the concentrated commercial short sellers.)

Even though he may have sold out early, the fact that Buffett did own silver once, and the fact that he admitted it offered unique investment capabilities due to its industrial deficit, points to silver's ability to outperform gold.

There is another billionaire out there, I should point out who, though less well known than Warren Buffett, also began to do his part for the silver story about 10 years ago. His name is Hugo Salinas Price and he lives in Mexico City. In the early 2000s, Salinas Price began a campaign to introduce silver coinage back into circulation in Mexico.

(More on this below) More than once, his proposal almost passed, and you can find information on these legislative efforts to bring back silver at plata.com.mx.

The Rise of SLV, and other online Silver Investments

The two reporting agencies who make it their business to understand the silver market both believe that 2006 was a very important year for silver due to the introduction of the iShares Silver Trust (SLV). This trust is currently the largest depository of silver in the world, larger than any government. Because many investment officers (for example pension funds or endowments) were forbidden from buying silver directly, the SLV allowed greater access for many to the price of silver. Not surprisingly, after 2006 there were more buyers than sellers in the silver market for the first time in over 16 years.

The second largest paper silver investment trust is the Central Fund of Canada (CEF), which is a closed end fund that invests in both silver and gold. It has been around since 1961. Other silver-only trusts or exchange traded funds have come into existence in recent years. The Zurich Cantonal Bank's silver ETF (ZSIL) is a large silver trust based in Switzerland, founded in 2007. Then there is the Sprott Physical Silver Trust (PSLV), launched in 2010, as well as the ETF Securities' Silver ETF (PHAG), based in London, founded in 2007. Besides these funds, there are other online precious metal firms, like goldmoney.com (founded in 2001) as well as bullionvault.com, founded in 2005, and silversaver.com.

Whatever you think of investing in silver through a brokerage account or through some other online repository (and therefore not taking delivery of it) you need to realize that the recent increase in these kinds of silver investment vehicles has played a large part in the rise of silver since 2006. Unprecedented numbers of investors can now gain access to silver without the difficulties associated with taking direct, personal delivery of metal.

Comparing the Current Silver Bull Market to the Last One

The last bull market in silver took the price of the white metal from a low of 26 cents in 1932 to a high in 1980 of nearly 50 dollars. I would divide the last silver bull market into two phases. The first phase, from 1932 to 1963, was driven almost entirely from industrial demand. This was the period in time when the pace of growth in electronics, appliances, and photography solidified the idea of silver as an industrial metal. Over this period, most estimates claim that industrial demand grew at a rate of 8-10% a year. We have yet to see such explosive growth in industrial demand. (Although as I will write later, there is a possibility of a reprise of silver's industrial revolution in the future due to alternative energy.)

But remember the important difference between this first period of silver's last bull market and the one today. Americans (and most people around the world) were forbidden from buying silver bullion from 1932 to 1963.

During the second phase of the last silver bull, from 1963 to 1980, investors were able to purchase silver bullion. But importantly, industrial demand actually began to decline in 1973, meaning that in the last bull market, you only had both industrial and investment demand pushing the silver price higher for about 10 years of the 50 years during which the price of silver was appreciating.

In terms of many metrics, when you compare this silver bull market to the last one (at least since 1960- I couldn't find the earlier data), things look more bullish for the metal in this bull market than during the end of the last one.

Industrial Demand: If we take a look back at the decade from 1971 to 1981, where silver soared (on average) from about 2 dollars to 18 or so, we see that industrial demand actually FELL on average by 3%, according to the World Silver Survey.[42] In fact, industrial demand actually peaked in 1973 at over 400 million ounces, and yet the silver price was only beginning to rocket higher from investment demand.

Recycling: Between 2000 and 2010, the average annual increase in silver recycling was 3.3%, according to data from the CPM Group. This should be contrasted to the period from 1960 to 1980, which saw annual average increases of 13%![43]

Increases in other supply: This is the really amazing part of the comparison between the bull market of the last ten years, and the bull market seen in the 1960s and 1970s. Remember that there were hundreds of millions of ounces of silver that could be dumped on investors during the last silver bull market. Just looking at U.S. Treasury sales alone, nearly 2 billion ounces of silver were sold from 1960 to 1980. This average amount of 100 million ounces represented over 25% of the mine supply for many of the years during those two decades.

Mine Supply Increases: This is the only area where the amount of change today is similar to the period from roughly 1960 to 1980. Average annual increases since 2010 have been around 2.5-3%, and this is almost exactly the increase seen over the course of the 60s and 70s.

Silver Is Rarer Today Then At Most Any Time in World History

Any discussion of silver today needs to acknowledge how the metal is much rarer today than in earlier eras, and also how silver production, while still growing, is nonetheless far less robust than it once was:

Peak growth rate in silver mine production (per 100 year time frame)

Many economic historians believe that the peak growth rate in silver mine production occurred way back in the 1500s, with the Spanish conquests of Mexico and Peru. Mine production leapt up at least 15 times, from 1 to 15 million ounces, or roughly a 12% annual growth rate in mining over the course of that century.[44] This growth rate was even higher than that between 1860 and 1940, when mine production increased from under 35 million ounces to over 275 million ounces, or about an 8% annual increase in mine production. Since 1940, increases in mine production have fallen off dramatically, to between 2 and 4% per year. The other amazing point about the New World silver discoveries is that some 500 years later, Mexico, Peru, and

Bolivia are almost always among the top two silver producers in the world.

Peak ratio of annual silver to gold production (in terms of silver's abundance)

According to monetary historians, the peak in the silver to gold mine ratio did not happen in the 1500s (although it was still high at around 25 to 1), but rather came during silver's industrial revolution from roughly 1885 to 1930. It reached a peak of nearly 40 to 1 around 1890, and was still as high as 30 to 1 in 1930.[45] According to Roy Jastram, there was a massive surplus of silver in the United States for industrial use in the early 1930s- a difference of five times.[46] We have never experienced this kind of silver surplus, or this large of an amount of mined silver compared to gold since. Currently, the production ratio of silver to gold is around 9 to 1, although this is not as low as the 5 to 1 ratio seen in the 1950s. And I don't need to tell you that the surplus in silver production is only a fraction of what it was in the 1930s.

Peak ratio of silver to world population

According to data compiled by the CPM Group, there were 3.25 billion ounces of silver above ground when Columbus discovered the New World in the 1490. With a world population of 400 million, there were over 8 ounces of silver for every person on the globe. This amount grew slightly in the 1500s, but so did world population, and when silver production peaked in 1600, the number of silver ounces per person was still in the 8-10 range. In 1700, there may have been as many as 4 billion ounces of silver above ground in the world. But the world population had grown faster than silver mine supply, by 50% since 1500, to 600 million people. So there were less than 7 ounces of silver per person on the planet. Today—even including jewelry–there are less than 4 silver ounces per person on planet Earth. If we just focus on coins and bullion, each person in the world can only have about .15 (fifteen hundredths) of an ounce of silver.[47]

Peak inflation-adjusted price of silver

Thinking of silver in relation to the monetary base is not the only way to evaluate what the "real" price of silver has been in past years and centuries. Roy Jastram, who authored *Silver- The Restless Metal* in 1980, felt that the value of silver in the 14th century was over 10 times higher than the average price in 1980 (the average price in 1980 was around 20 dollars.) He calculated this by looking at the relative purchasing power of silver compared to a basket of commodities. The average price of silver over the course of the prior 1000 years has moved as follows: 700 over the course of the 16th century, 500 dollars over the course of the 17th century; 400 dollars in the 18th century and then it began its slide in the 19th century down below 10 dollars in the 20th century.[48] Remember that, depending upon your definition of inflation, the relationships established by Jastram would be even greater today. The peak price in silver would be a minimum of 600 dollars and likely over 1000 dollars in 2012 dollars.

Peak percentage of primary silver production versus byproduct of other metals

While no one can know for certain, the highest percentage of primary silver production was likely 50%, and probably achieved in the pre-modern era. Silver has always been known as a byproduct of gold and lead, but before the nineteenth century, the technology did not yet exist to extract silver in large amounts from the base metals. So primary silver production formed a much higher percentage of overall silver mine supply many centuries ago than it does today.

Peak amount of silver held at futures exchanges

Another way of thinking about peak silver is to ask about silver supplies at the major futures exchanges. The amount of silver under the control of the four largest futures exchanges, the COMEX, the Chicago Board of Trade, the London Metal Exchange, and the Tokyo Metals Exchange peaked at 350 million ounces in 1992, with the vast majority, nearly 280 million being at the COMEX.[49] Today? The number has declined to below 150 million ounces, as of 2011 (the London Metal Exchange also no longer offers silver futures trading.) Today's number is lower than 1972, by the way, even though there are many more ounces of paper silver trading than in 1972, not long after silver futures trading was legalized by the US and British governments in 1964 and 1968, respectively.

In many ways, silver is a metal whose true rarity in not appreciated by many--- but I have to wonder for how much longer that will remain the case.

Chapter 5
What's Driving Silver Investment?

Seven Possible Reasons for Higher Silver Prices

Historians often talk about recipes, or a combination of factors that cause a certain event to happen in history (for example, the stock market crash of 1929). Normally more than one factor plays a role in bringing about a certain event—it is a case of several factors creating a result larger than the sum of their parts. Or, alternatively, there are so many reasons for something to possibly occur, that it dramatically increases the chance that the event will in fact come to pass.

With silver, there is not only one reason for the price to move higher, but (at least) seven that I can think of. And please also note that not all of these reasons have to do with a currency collapse or other financial mishap—as I have tried to explain, the silver story, while partly about crisis investing, is about much more.

So here are seven possible reasons for higher silver prices:

1) Financial Repression Encouraging a Move into Hard (or Real) Assets

The concept of financial repression has been popularized by Carmen Reinhart and Ken Rogoff. They point out for nearly 35 years after World War II (from 1945 to 1980), western nations needed to suppress interest rates (and therefore steal from savers through inflation) in order to reduce debt loads.

The current zero percent interest rate policy is a return to financial repression. Savers have not yet begun to move significant amounts of savings out of the paper system and into real assets, but if they did, you should remember where the price of silver went between 1945 and 1980: from roughly 50 cents, to (briefly) 50 dollars.[1]

2) Dramatic Increases in Silver Industrial Demand
If the demand for silver for industrial uses were to start increasing by a faster rate than over the past 20 years (about 4% a year, give or take), the silver price would begin a faster rate of ascent than what is seen currently.

3) Peak Silver or Mine Supply Disruption
If silver production were to stop increasing, or even to decrease, you would have serious supply pressures on the metal that could only be resolved with higher prices (if even that). Such a situation could occur because of resource scarcity, political troubles in silver producing countries, economic depression, or war.

4) Remonetization of Silver/ Rebuilding of Official Stockpiles
As I have mentioned several times in this book, silver is no longer held in any significant amount by central banks (for monetary purposes) or by governments (for strategic purposes.) If that were to change, once again you would see a whole new price range for the white metal. The same is true if a large enough number of average people decided to use silver in everyday transactions.

5) Gold-only investors diversifying into silver
Since the value of the world's investable silver is only about 5% the value of its investable gold, if those who only own

gold diversified even 5% into the silver market, the price of silver could double in value without any new silver investors entering the market. This could happen, especially if gold-only investors realized how mispriced silver is relative to above-ground supply (an important point I'll come back to below.)

6) The End of the Paper Silver Short Concentration at the COMEX
If, for whatever reason, the large short paper short positions by the four largest traders (meaning paper sales by banks) were to be reduced, the price of silver could also move dramatically higher, since it is not clear who would have firepower like the large banks to supply unbacked paper silver in the amounts done by large short sellers recently. Similarly, if a long-side concentration like the Hunts were to reoccur, silver prices would also quickly move up.

7) Loss of Investor Confidence/ The Social Movement Wildcard
Obviously in a crisis moment either for the US Dollar, or some other western currency, due to the enormous amount of debt racked up by these nations, hard assets (like silver) are going to outperform stocks. Moreover, it is important to note that it does not take many people to believe that they are having a currency crisis, or that they need to make a statement with ownership of physical metal, for the price of silver to rise dramatically. This is what I call the social movement wildcard, where people express their frustration at the current monetary system through investing in silver. We only need about 500,000 or 1 million people *in the world* to try to buy about 50,000 dollars worth of actual, physical silver for the price to explode in value by several times. Or,

given how cheap silver is, if 500 million people tried to buy 4 ounces of silver (roughly 130 dollars as of mid-2012) the silver does not exist. It is not a case of the metal not being for sale—it simply is not there.

Thinking like a child: why is silver so cheap?

For some reason, going way back to when I was practically in diapers, I was fascinated by shiny stones and coins. Its hard to know why, except that if you share my addiction, you understand the attraction to things like gold, silver, or rare stones; items that in many cases have truly stood the test of time, and that can't be destroyed by disasters- either natural or manmade. These are the items that truly last. Maybe that is why I wanted them, or understood or appreciated them. In a disposable world, where everything from your kitchen appliances to your computer, to your marriage can be thrown away, I can understand people wanting something that is unchanging, permanent. This is an important reason people are drawn to hard assets. Some people are innately skeptical regarding paper investments—I guess it comes down to the old adage that if you can't touch it or see it, you don't really own it.

Knowing that I liked old coins so much, my granddad would sometimes share some of his collection of pre-1964 silver from when he worked at a bank. It was from him that I learned about Gresham's Law, or the idea that bad money drives out good (people hoard silver coins when they are replaced with cheaper metal). At the time (early 1980s) I understood that these coins were maybe 5 or 10 dollars- maybe 15 in some cases, and I knew that these coins were worth about as much as other toys or video games, or even books that I might want. But I wondered why I wasn't receiving any gold coins. The silver coin looked pretty nice to me, it had been money once, but had become too rare for one reason or another to still be treated as legal tender (under most circumstances). So pushing my luck, I asked my dad as a hint that I would like to have a gold coin for some holiday or other. I was politely told (and given a look like "don't get greedy kid") that gold was SIXTY OR SEVENTY TIMES more expensive than silver—meaning that the gold version of the silver coins I had went for as high as 450 dollars.

To be honest, I must have intuitively already understood that gold would be a little pricier than silver. I understood from athletic competitions that gold stands for first place, silver for second, or from any number of other examples that gold was "the metal of kings" so it wasn't exactly like I thought that silver and gold would be equal in price. But 450 dollars versus 8?? What was this about? What was worse, my dad couldn't seem to give me an answer as to why silver was so much cheaper than gold, except for what I just wrote- everybody seems to agree that silver is a distant second to gold. It was only later that I learned that banks still hold gold and that super rich people prefer holding gold. But this fact also meant that the silver market was pretty tiny and might possess the fuel to take off in an explosive way if enough people woke up and began buying in bulk.

I bring up this story to remind people that it is important to think like a child. When something doesn't look quite right, when it looks like the adults probably have something wrong, you may want to trust you inner child more than the adult who has learned to accept the world as it is. Yes, silver is not the go-to money of central bankers or the uber-rich. But at a time when so much else is in flux in our world, when so many people are questioning long-held assumptions (like the idea that depressions never happen- or the idea of the dollar as the dominant currency for world trade) you may want to try questioning this other time-honored tradition as well: that the market will always value silver substantially less than gold. Just a thought. Silver is every bit a monetary metal as is gold- and has been for thousands of years. They both stand the test of time when paper currencies lose their value. One just happens to be a lot cheaper than the other—at least for now.

Physical Ratios Between Gold and Silver

As of early 2012, the market price of silver was over 50 times cheaper than gold. The main reason for this, as mentioned above, is due to the favored status gold has with governments or wealthy individuals. But in terms of physical supply, you need to understand that this ratio of 50 to 1 bears no relationship to reality. Some people will tell you that the "natural" ratio for gold and silver is about 15-20 to 1, but they are either referring to an arbitrary monetary ratio that once existed (see above), or they are referring to what geologists believe to be the natural occurrence of these metals in all parts of the Earth. The problem with the natural occurrence ratio, is that miners cannot get to all of this metal. More useful are the following ratios, which I think bear a stronger resemblance to reality:

9:1 is the ratio of silver to gold annual mine production[2]

10:1 is the estimated ratio of economic gold to silver in the ground[3]

5:1 is the estimated physical ratio of all silverware, silver/gold jewelry and other stocks above ground[4]

1:3 (less gold than silver) is the physical ratio of gold and silver coins/bullion[5]

Crisis Consciousness

I've already mentioned the phrase "investment realism," meaning that people have got to understand that bad things can happen to good people. Its not about being neurotic, or a worrywart, or about hoping for bad things, or thinking that the world is going to end. No, it is just as simple as understanding the need to have all of your bases covered when something comes at you out of the blue. Let me give you a personal example. I mentioned earlier how I grew up in Orange County, CA. The neighborhood I grew up in had to deal with the threat of wildfires (our house was in danger from two of them); mudslides (several houses slid down a nearby hill when I was a small kid); earthquakes; and concerns about droughts as well as regarding a nuclear power plant at San Onofre, CA melting down (so far so good on that front.) It was drummed into my head that people needed to have supplies of food, water, emergency kits, or an emergency route in the event of evacuation. This should be common sense. But we all know how difficult it is for most people to actually be prepared. In my home region, people are often too busy living the good life, or thinking that only other people have to deal with the nastiness and unpleasantness of things breaking down. But I think that events of the last decade have reawakened a sense of preparedness in people, whether we are talking about natural disasters like Hurricane Katrina in 2005, or we are talking about the financial disasters like Madoff or MF Global.

Physical silver is monetary insurance. It goes right along with the supplies of water, or food, or fuel, or other necessities that people like me who live in earthquake zones are supposed to have, but often never have enough of. Buying silver does not mean you think the world is going to end. It simply means that you have sized up certain risks around you, and are taking some small steps to try to prudently manage your savings, and possibly give yourself peace of mind when you sleep at night.

I think the act of remembering all of the stupid illegal [insert expletives of choice] from the past 10 years will also make you remember why people buy silver. Silver, the investment whose math does not add up in a crisis. Even at 1.7 billion ounces, the number of people who can have even one 715 ounce bag of "junk" silver coinage (or bullion equivalent) is less than 2.5 million people on planet earth. This bag, although heavy, fits in a shoebox (it is just hard to carry that way). 715 ounces is not really a lot of silver, and it only costs about 20,000 dollars. For those who are savers out there- yes, they do exist- 20,000 dollars is not that much money, especially if you are trying to insure a six or seven or eight figure net worth. And so there would be many people who would try to get more than 715 ounces, but for everyone who does that, there is that much less silver for someone else to get their hands on. There would be much less for any ETF or other trust to own. There would also be less silver for any government that decided to restock its supply of silver bullion. So I would bet that the real number of people who can own a shoebox of silver in physical form is well below 1 million people in the world, perhaps as low as 500,000. The reason the silver price has been moving higher (at least in part) is due to this basic mathematical problem—there is not enough monetary insurance to go around. Period

David Morgan once wrote an article about "silver millionaires." His point was how few people can actually physically own one million dollars worth of silver. Let me explain why. According to Merrill Lynch, there are anywhere between 10-20 million people (or households) on the planet that have a net worth of 1 million dollars.[6] How many of these millionaires could put even 1 million dollars into silver coins and bullion? (At 40 dollars an ounce, one million dollars in silver is roughly 25,000 ounces). Only about 50,000 people (or households) in the world could buy roughly 1 million dollars of silver, and this would mean that no one else could own any silver coins or bullion at all. If just 3 percent (600,000) of the 20 million millionaires in the world tried to shift even 80,000 dollars into silver (2500 ounces), they would buy up roughly all of the silver coins and bullion known to exist on the planet, leaving none for anyone poorer (or richer) than themselves.

Where are the number of millionaires growing fastest? Asia, of course. According to the same research, the number of millionaires on that continent grew nearly 10 percent in 2010, to over 3.3 million people. It is estimated that there may be anywhere from 15-30 million additional people in the world with between 500,000 and 1 million dollar in wealth, which is another category of individuals who might buy silver.[7]

Inflation Consciousness

Yes, a big driver of silver investment over the last several years has been related to the bull market in survivalism. People are looking over their shoulder, hoping for the best, but expecting the worst. This reason reflects the darkening social mood, as many in the western world face an uncertain financial future. However, this concern is also why so many people have purchased bonds, like US Treasuries. It is more out of a concern regarding asset deflation, then it is a concern about the possibility that the ultra-accommodative monetary policies of central banks might actually succeed in setting off serious inflation. Many have noted the bubble in the bond market, and wonder how much longer all of this capital will stay in an investment that while safe, does not protect well against inflation.

If you lived through the 1970s, you understand that inflation-consciousness certainly kicked in at a time when interest rates steadily marched upward. People, financial institutions, even governments did not believe that they were being sufficiently compensated for the risk of investing in government debt. I can't guarantee when, but when we look at events in Europe in 2011, it certainly seems possible that rising rates could impact wealthier countries, either in Western Europe, or America. I won't even go into possible scenarios in Europe when or if nations break away from the Euro- their citizens will immediately lose purchasing power when their bank deposits are reconverted into former currencies such as the drachma or the lira.

Some who are not fans of the gold and silver bugs like to claim that gold and silverbugs refer to the precious metals as "safe havens." They mockingly point to this whenever the price of gold and silver drops in the paper futures markets as if to say- see, you idiot goldbugs- your "safe" investment isn't so safe after all because its nominal value can bounce all over the place—or even go down.

As with so much else, the conventional paper bugs, as I like to call them, completely miss the point about gold and silver investing, at least as far as I'm concerned. Why? Because I invest in gold and silver precisely out of the conviction that *nothing* is truly safe in this world, not only stocks, real estate, or bonds- but yes, even what the system refers to as "cash," meaning bank deposits or short term government bonds. Yes, even "cash" is not safe from currency devaluation, debasement- in short- the inflation tax. You think that just because the value of your bank account or short term bond does not change that you haven't lost money? You couldn't be more wrong.

If gold or silver bugs are incredulous when faced with the majority of people who own no gold or silver and claim to like it that way, it is because we feel that not owning gold and silver is simply irresponsible when faced with politicians or others who are trying their best to inflate away the value of debts (not that they will necessarily succeed.) Not owning gold or silver is as irresponsible as not having extra food in the event of a snowstorm, or as dumb as not having flashlights and water in the event of some other natural disaster.

The Five Myths of Silver Investing

There are also several myths about silver that may lead some people to claim that the metal is fairly valued, or even overvalued at the moment. I happen to believe that silver is actually quite cheap. I think there are several misconceptions about silver that need to be put to rest.

Of course I understand that markets do not often trade on fundamentals, or at least they don't for years at a time. There is the old adage that "markets can stay irrational longer than you can remain solvent," and this is meant to show how stupid, frankly, many people can be when it comes to investing or speculating with money. However, if anyone tells you that silver is overpriced base on some reason having to do with mine supply, aboveground stockpiles, or even economic growth, you should remember what I said above: silver is not priced on its fundamentals. It is priced on the misconceptions and false beliefs of investors, both big and small.

There are at least five major myths about silver investing. Let me briefly go over some of them:

1. Silver is an "economically sensitive" metal

During the recession of 2008-2009, the CPM Group estimated that silver demand from photography, jewelry, and industry dropped by roughly 80 million ounces. Mine supply also increased by about 30 million ounces, along with a 15 million or so increase in recycling. So in order for the price of silver to remain stable (theoretically), you would need investors to make up this roughly 100 million ounce difference, which is exactly what they did. Given the fact that people understood the need to buy precious metals during a banking crisis, investment demand for silver increased by nearly 100 million ounces at the same time as demand fell and other sources of silver also increased.[8]

Over the course of 2008 and 2009, the silver price more or less remained stable, even as it saw wild swings induced by paper trading. So, during one of the worst recessions in modern memory, real, physical demand for silver cancelled out declining industrial use. An important point to remember when someone tells you the silver price is destined to go down in the next recession.

2. Silver coins and bullion are more plentiful than gold

In fact, it is the exact opposite. Being generous (and using data from the CPM Group as well as the Silver Institute) there are maybe 1.7 billion ounces of silver coin and bullion in the world, versus roughly 3 billion ounces of gold coins and bullion. Yes, it is true that recently about 80 million more ounces of silver bullion/coins are produced each year than gold, but that still means that it will take over 15 years before the silver stockpile in the world even equals that of gold, let alone becomes greater. So why is the price of silver roughly 50 times cheaper than gold? Good question.[9]

3. The high price of silver will drive down demand from industry

This one has had no basis in fact for the period from 2000 to 2010. During that decade, industrial demand, according to most estimates, basically remained flat.[10] This is amazing, when you consider that the price of silver went from 4 dollars to over 20 in that period. But because silver is used in such small amounts in things like electronics and solar panels, increasing silver costs have yet to dampen demand for highly desired toys like computers and cell phones. And many silver experts believe that such demand will only increase in the years ahead. You should realize that a rising silver price does not seem to dampen industrial demand.

4. At the right price, billions of ounces of silver will get recycled

Many do believe that there are nearly 6 times as many ounces of silver jewelry (and silverware) than gold jewelry in the world. So you might think that there is a lot of silver that will get melted down someday. One problem with this argument is that much of this silver either a) costs way more than even the current bullion spot price and b) is held in very small amounts all over the world by millions of people (oftentimes women). They won't care to sell for a very long time—if ever.

But there is an even more important point here. I bet most people who claim to follow the precious metals don't realize that as of 2010, we had yet to see more silver recycled than during 1980. That is thirty years of silver recycling more or less going nowhere, even as the price of silver spent more time above 20 dollars an ounce in 2010 than in 1980. I am going to be optimistic and guess that we will finally best the old recycling high this year in silver (at over 300 million ounces). But in a world where 300 million ounces of silver is only 10 billion dollars, and in a world where investors are slated to purchase nearly that much silver in physical form over the next couple of years, you really have to wonder why anyone would think there is all of this silver just lying around ready to be brought to the market to cool off silver's price. And given what I said about how impervious industrial demand is to silver price increases, a lot of whatever silver jewelry gets recycled will be used and consumed by industry (even assuming that preservation techniques get better as the price goes higher.)

I also would not expect mine increases to somehow meet demand: few industry experts believe silver can increase more than 4 or 5 percent a year (roughly 50 million ounces, or less than 2 billion dollars), especially when nearly 80% of silver is a byproduct of metals like copper, lead, and zinc.

5. Retail silver investors are fickle/ there is no plan to remonetize silver

This myth had some basis in truth, at least according to the experts who tracked silver buying and selling activity in the 1980s and 1990s (such as the CPM Group or Silver Institute). Many agree that retail investors (probably following the lead of governments) sold far more silver than gold during the twenty years between 1985 and 2005. Probably to the tune of over 1 billion ounces. So many felt that silver investors were flakes who really didn't have the staying power of gold investors. Or, as I mentioned above, it may have just been the case that average investors followed the lead of governments, since those governments dumped far more silver than gold during the same period (gold is the only precious metal held by central banks, in addition).[11]

But in recent years, I am struck by how many proposals there are like the one from Hugo Salinas Price in Mexico attempting to bring back silver coins into the market in his country. Then we have all of the state legislation in the United States aiming to bring back both gold and silver into economic transactions. Remember, silver is perceived to be the money of average people (even as it is rarer than gold) so any grassroots effort to bring back precious metals into everyday transactions will dramatically increase silver's value. We have already seen the amazing turnaround in silver retail investment buying over the past few years (hundreds of millions of new ounces) and I think some people are slowly waking up to how undervalued silver is. But believe it or not, many, many more have yet to do so.

Silver Price Suppression

You may not want to be a commodity speculator, and I understand that. However, at times like these, where Central Banks are telling you that "cash is trash," and where savers are under attack, you have been conscripted into the Army of Speculators whether you like it or not (assuming you actually want to grow your savings.) Given this fact, you have to understand all aspects of a given market, or why a price is set, or how it moves in all respects. In the case of silver, in addition to all of the strong fundamentals I can and will list, there is another possibility, that of a short squeeze in this market. Understand that commodity markets are often knocked around by big players, or entities who think that they own an entire market. This can be a bank or a billionaire (like the Hunts, for example.) This is just a fact, and a realistic assessment of any market. At the moment, the big concentration is on the "short" side of silver, and many have wondered if, at some point, these shorts may give up, or "cover" their positions. When they do so, it is unclear if anyone else will be able to fill their shoes to keep the price of silver "under control." Many suspect that the resulting short squeeze will only further gain the attention of the investing public, and result in the mother of all price explosions to the upside for the white metal.

Tectonic Shifts, Bank Runs, and the COMEX

2008 was also eye-opening because of how the price of paper silver and gold behaved during a crisis widely seen as the worst since the Great Depression. The behavior of silver prices in particular exposed the weakness of the main price discovery mechanism, the COMEX division of the New

York Mercantile exchange. Put another way, the physical market revealed that the most common way to price silver will not always be in control. You have to understand that historically whenever there was concern about the solvency of banks (or governments), large investors scrambled for gold and silver. We know this because during times of crisis, large investors or banks, would pay a premium above the official government price of the precious metals due to concern about their financial future. Sometimes, these premiums could be as high as 100% above the fixed price.

What was so surprising to me about the price of gold and-especially silver- in the period from March 2008 to March 2009 was the ability of the paper price to get knocked down, and knocked down hard. At one point, the paper price of gold dropped some 30% from 1000 dollars an ounce in March of 2008, to a low of around 700 dollars in November. Silver went on an even wilder ride, dropping from its March high of 20 dollars to below 9 dollars by the fall of 2008, a drop of over 50%.

But this was not the only thing that caught my eye: what was more striking was the reaction of the physical market to these paper developments. As a coin collector, it was amazing to watch the premiums on some coins explode anywhere from 20-80% above the price being quoted on the exchange (this was particularly true for generic U.S. gold coins from before 1933). Dealers and other large buyers were reporting large delays- up to six months- for the delivery of gold or silver orders. The reason for the delays, as far as I'm concerned, originated because the paper markets had mispriced the asset far below what real people in real time were willing to pay for actual, physical metal. This was an even more important clue that something was wrong with the paper precious metals markets (and especially the silver market.)

So what happened on the paper markets? Why were they so distorted from the physical price? What does this mean about the way the metals are priced (largely in New York)? More importantly, was there some sort of conspiracy or illegal activity knocking the price down at a time of severe financial stress?

Perhaps like others who follow the bullion or coin markets, this experience opened up a lot of questions regarding what is called "price discovery" in the world of finance. You know, the idea that we have a free and fair market, that when you open up a market to lots of buyers and sellers, you will come up with a better price than if the government or some other large entity were to set the price. Many financial professionals will tell you how the "price discovery" mechanisms that exist today further the ends of free and fair markets. But after having seen some of the dislocations caused by 2008, I would beg to differ.

As it turns out, in the case of silver, the paper trading is anywhere from 100-200 times the underlying metal.[12] You read that correctly- at an institution like the COMEX- very little physical silver trades hands, and yet this institution usually sets the price of the metal- as it did when the paper "price" crashed in 2008 before physical buyers swamped the market.

The COMEX silver market, to me, is a derivative of silver. I don't quite mean this in the sense that they are unregulated bets—but I do mean to say that the amount of paper silver trading only seems to grow far and above beyond the growth in mining supply or available bullion stockpiles. One of the more important points about the silver market is that unlike almost any other market for

153

commodities, there is less physical supply available today than 40 years ago, but many times more paper investment vehicles, or ways to play the market.

To go back to one of the earliest years leveraged futures contracts traded on the COMEX (1969), the exchange had roughly 115 million ounces of silver in total, but traded 6.6 billion ounces for the year.[13] By 1984 it had increased to nearly 34 billion ounces.[14] And by 2009 it had increased to over 50 billion ounces.[15] So there were nearly ten times as many paper ounces traded in 2009 than in 1969 at the COMEX, but slightly fewer ounces held at the exchange. Moreover, according to the CPM Group, total silver trading for the London Bullion Market Association was an additional 30 billion ounces.[16] The data from London has only been released since the 1990s, but it reveals that paper trading accounts for over 100 billion, with a 'b' ounces....Is it really possible that this much physical silver is moving around the world and needs to somehow be hedged by a dealer? Even though silver mine supplies have increased from roughly 250 million ounces to 600 million ounces, over the same time period, silver bullion stockpiles have actually declined by over 40%, from over 2.5 billion ounces to about 1.7 billion. So there really isn't that much silver around that needs to be hedged by producers. And even compared to the increases in mine production, the increases in paper silver (at over 10 TIMES)- look silly. It is possible that physical trading of silver has increased around the globe since 1980, but ten times as much *physical* trading? It looks to many as though all of this paper silver serves no purpose other than to increase the bottom line of the exchanges catering to various forms of speculators.

Since silver has been turned into a commodity future by the powers that be, it is important to back up and explain where these futures "markets" come from, how they have grown, and how we arrived at such an unstable point in the silver market.

A futures market originated as a way for producers of a certain commodity (say, wheat) to be able to "hedge" future price decreases. This idea of hedging is basically an insurance policy. In nineteenth century America, it was noted that at the end of the crop year, farmers would flood the market with grain, and prices would drop dramatically. Grain would be left to rot, or would be dumped, which depressed prices and in turn discouraged others from growing or transporting grain to market. As a result, buyers and sellers sought to provide for their needs by contracting for the delivery of certain quantities at a certain specific date in the future. You can think of this as a way of locking in a guaranteed price before making the journey to market. In the United States, Chicago was the focus of much of the nineteenth century futures market due to its proximity to farms. By 1864 there were trading pits at the exchange, and thus began the Chicago Board of Trade.

However, almost immediately, it became clear that many people were trading in futures as speculative bets on the price. Worse, there were numerous reports of individuals trying to corner a given market, meaning they would buy up all the supply and try to push prices ever higher. There were several men in the late nineteenth century known as "wheat kings" or "corn kings" because of their manipulative attempts to push prices around in the direction they wanted.

In the case of one William Sturgess, he racked up huge unpaid debts to the exchange but he was not alone- as a result, the Chicago Board of Trade went to the Illinois State Legislature and convinced that body to pass an anti-corner statute.[17] However people only needed to state their "intention" to take delivery of a certain commodity in order to avoid this law—and to continue gambling.

From the beginning of commodity futures markets in the United States, then, there have been accusations of unfair manipulative concentrations, and more than several complaints about the players in futures being nothing more than gamblers. Moreover, as outlined above, governments have been trying to regulate these futures markets since the nineteenth century. Of course, the federal government has also suspended trading altogether in certain commodities when it has been deemed in the national interest. Several commodities- among them wheat- were suspended during World War I so as to prevent speculators from taking advantage of shortages or disruptions related to war. The same occurred during World War II. Additionally, certain commodities, such as eggs, at one time could be traded on paper in the futures markets, but trading has since been suspended (in the case of eggs this suspension occurred in the 1970s.)[18]

When the federal government was not closing down futures markets, they were investigating them. In 1920, there was an investigation by the Federal Trade Commission into the collapse of wheat prices. The commission determined that there should be taxes on wheat trading not done on government approved exchanges. Congress also noted how many banks were embroiled in overextended loans to gamblers on futures exchanges.[19] Over time, the federal government tried to increase its oversight of futures markets.

The Commodity Exchange Act of 1936 is the origin of public reporting requirements regarding which traders are taking what positions (as well as how many positions) in a given market. It was also around this time that the Department of Agriculture published an amusing report regarding the occupations and backgrounds of individuals involved in futures trading. It found that the traders included 6 dead men, 18 undertakers, 2 butlers, 5 chauffeurs, 6 janitors, 12 candy store proprietors, 1 clam digger, some 25 assorted clergymen, 1 dilletente, one individual "who just fizzles around", 1 duck raiser, 3 police chiefs, 3 senators, 36 students, 4 unemployed widows, and 1,025 housewives![20] Who knows how serious this data is, but it certainly left the impression that, as President Harry Truman later stated, most people involved in the grain markets were simply gamblers and that Americans should not be held hostage "to the greed of speculators."[21]

But concentrations, squeezes, and corners continued to plague the commodity markets. In the case of the 1960s, there was the "salad oil king," Anthony De Angelis, who used proceeds from a fraudulent soybean and cottonseed oil warehouse to attempt to corner the market in soybeans. DeAngelis got loans from large banks like Bank of America and Chase Manhattan, but when his scam was uncovered it led to several hundred million dollars in losses, the bankruptcy of sixteen companies, as well as jail time for DeAngelis. In response to scams and Ponzi schemes like these, there were increasing calls for more government oversight, though as we will see, crooks and cartels seem to find a way around the regulators.

Be that as it may, several other scandals later led to the creation of the Commodity Futures Trade Commission in 1975. The stated purpose of the CFTC is to protect market users and the public from fraud, manipulation, and abusive practices related to the sale of commodity and financial futures and options. The commission also exists to supposedly foster open, competitive, and financially sound futures and option markets. But, like I said, complaints can still be heard. As with other commodities traded at places like the Chicago Board of Trade or the New York Mercantile Exchange, the amount of borrowing, or leverage in gold and silver markets has only increased relative to mine output or above ground stockpiles since the 1970s. When coupled with the concentration in positions held at the exchanges (in many commodities only a few institutions account anywhere from 30-60% of the trading volume) many believe that these markets are simply casinos for banks and other well connected Wall Street firms.

Silver's Next Industrial Revolution

Besides investor interest, or the interest of commodity speculators, there are the industrial uses for silver, uses which can also play a role in making silver more expensive in the years to come. Many will talk about silver only as an industrial metal which, as we've seen, misrepresents the metal's history as money. However, there is no doubt that industrial demand for this metal has exploded before, and may very well do so again. When you think about the possibility of increasing demand for silver both from investors and industrial users, you can see why some people think that the price ratio of silver to gold could get awfully close one day to 1 to 1 (just to put that into perspective, this would mean that silver would have to rise over 50 *times* from present day values.)

In the period between roughly 1900 and 1970, industrial demand for silver increased over 4 times- from 100 million to 400 million ounces. The industrial revolution in silver was due largely to the urbanization and technological revolutions taking place in twentieth century life. Whether we are talking about indoor plumbing, electricity, cars, or aerospace technology, silver proved to be an indispensable metal. One of the largest industrial uses for silver came from photography, invented by Frenchmen Nicephore Niecpe in 1822, and made more popular by Daguerre in the 1840s. By the twentieth century millions of ounces of silver were needed just for photography. But in terms of silver demand, this was just the tip of the iceberg.[22]

Still, at some point around 1970, the industrial demand for silver stopped increasing (for a time it actually decreased.) Over the next several decades, industrial demand increases have been far smaller, after having reached the 400 million ounce level in 1970. During the last four years, industrial demand (including photography) has been around 550 million ounces annually. So you can see that the growth in industrial demand has slowed significantly over the last 40 years. But many in the silver industry think this could change, and that industrial silver demand could begin to move toward 800 million ounces a year, or even higher.

The reasons for this growth should not be hard to understand: silver is in many ways a more versatile industrial metal than copper. James Blanchard was fond of pointing out how the average American used several items with silver in it even before he or she left for work in the morning: silver is in your alarm clock, wall switch, wristwatch, bathroom mirror, the plumbing in your bathroom or kitchen, your microwave, water purifier, dishwasher, and, especially if you wear polyester, it is used to make many forms of clothing.[23]

Silver is used in computers and cell phones. Batteries need silver for their cathode or negative side. Silver oxide cells are used in cameras, toys, hearing aids, calculators, and even though they are expensive, silver oxide cells are seen as a more environmentally friendly version of the lithium-ion batteries used in everything from consumer electronics to electric cars. Silver electroplated steel ball bearings are used in jet engines, because the silver provides superior performance and lubrication in the event of an engine shutdown. Membrane switches, which require only a light touch, use silver, and these switches are now part of televisions, telephones, microwave ovens, and computer keyboards. Silver is used to coat CDs and DVDs because the white metal is resistant to pitting and tarnish. Silver is also useful in brazing and soldering- meaning in the joining together of materials, producing leak tight and corrosion resistant joints. Silver tin solders are used to bond copper pipes and faucets. Refrigerators also rely upon silver soldering and government regulations are mandating greater use of silver soldering, due to concerns regarding the toxicity of customary tin/lead solders.[24]

Although the vast majority of wiring uses copper, this is only because copper is so much cheaper than silver per ounce. Silver is an amazing conductor of electricity at practically any temperature, and it is possible that silver wiring may gain attention in the future. In the United States, HTS wiring carries over 140 times as much current as copper, and it is believed that this wiring is far better at preventing power surges or other inefficiencies which can lead to transmission losses within our power grid. HTS transformers are more environmentally friendly and don't use as much oil as their counterparts. Understand that HTS wiring is by no means prevalent, and may not be for a long time. But it is also important to note that as science and technology evolve, and as more and more countries move toward green technology, silver can play an even more important industrial role than at present.[25]

Silver is also a useful catalyst, especially in the creation of ethylene oxide and formaldehyde, both of which are essential chemicals for plastics, polyester clothing, adhesives, resins, scratch resistant coatings, and antifreeze coolant for automobiles and other vehicles. Because silver interrupts a bacteria cells ability to form chemical bonds needed to survive, silver is an excellent anti-bacterial agent. For this reason, silver is useful in hospitals trying to find equipment that can kill the MRSA (Methicillin-resistant Staphylococcus aureus) "superbug." Silver is also used in burn ointments.

Increased demand for silver as a medical-metal, or as a sanitizer can come from very high end uses. For example, it is now possible to embed silver in countertops, and possible to put it in clothing, even underwear (in addition to silver's uses in the production of other fibers). For a long time, the Indian sari contained some silver in it- this attests to the age-old desire for the white metal as a defense against disease. In addition to jewelry and silverware, silver can be used in horse saddles, or other equestrian equipment, and is also present in many musical instruments, ranging from bells to flutes.

But even in a severe recession, silver demand can move higher because there are so many non-luxury goods and gadgets that need silver now, or will need it in the future. For example, David Morgan has simply looked at applications for silver relating to food, water, and energy.

These are the three things people need the most, and they are three areas that will likely need a lot more silver regardless of prevailing economic conditions. These three areas will also contribute to increased silver demand in ways that cannot be easily recovered (at least for now.) Most people understand that many governments are pushing solar energy as an alternative to present energy sources. But solar energy uses silver, especially because silver paste is used in 90 percent of all crystalline silicon photovoltaic cells. If you live in the American Southwest, you have seen the growth in solar technology in order to help get homes and businesses off the power grid. Silver coated mirrors are also used to create scalding hot water, which then becomes steam and is used to run electric generators.

From these kinds of uses for silver, experts predict the possibility of an additional 80 to 100 million ounces of silver demand per year. As of this writing, much of this silver is unrecoverable, meaning that it will likely be consumed. Another area of strong demand will come from newer water purification systems that are employing silver instead of more toxic chemicals such as chlorine and bromine. In pools and spas silver ion canisters can spread a biocide blanket easily to ward off disease. Silver is also used in personal water purification tubes as well. David Morgan is also impressed with the possible uses of silver in food processing- particularly in packaging. With nanotechnology, you can impregnate silver into plastic sheets as a way of keeping bacteria out. Silver for RFID tags (a scanning device used to replace bar codes) will be needed to put these tags in cars, bank debit cards, or casino chips, and could also push industrial demand dramatically higher.[26]

Because of all of these new industrial uses for silver, some experts believe that silver will be moving back into a deficit situation, meaning that more above ground stockpiles will have to be consumed to meet demand and the above ground stock of silver will once again decline. Put another way, there are several possible reasons- in addition to investment demand- that could allow for silver prices to explode. It is true that jewelry scrapping could increase to fill the deficit, and that jewelry demand could decline. It is also possible that recycling could eventually increase. But these factors may not yield any more than 100-200 million ounces of silver in a given year- or 5 or 10 billion dollars at 2011 prices. And investors may very well stand in to make up the difference, since silver is still so much cheaper than gold, therefore eliminating the benefits to supply from declining jewelry production and increased recycling.

Silver bulls like Morgan, as well as Izzy Friedman and Ted Butler wonder if there might not be a moment when silver industrial users hit the panic button and drive silver dramatically higher, as they try to get their hands on an asset that is also sought after as an investment hedge by millions of retail investors. This industrial panic could far exceed the one for palladium in 2000. In that year, Ford Motor Company feared a shortage and bought large amounts of palladium in response to disruptions coming out of Russia, one of the world's largest palladium producers. The price of palladium skyrocketed to nearly 1100 dollars an ounce, or over 3 times the price of just 18 months earlier. And this occurred to a metal that had limited investor interest: it was all about the industrial users getting scared and scrambling to buy whatever they could. Silver, which is more versatile and cheaper than palladium-- and which has a history of being a monetary metal-- could see a much larger price spike due to its industrial *and* monetary or investment uses.

Here's A Small List of Items Using Silver:

Air-conditioners
Adhesives
Anti-freeze
Automobiles
Batteries (especially silver oxide zinc batteries)
Bearings in jet engines
Cameras
Cell Phones
Clothing
Compact Disks (some, though not all)
Computers
Dental Fillings
Dishwashers
Eyeglasses
Hearing Aids
Jewelry
Microwaves
Mirrors
Packaging Materials
Photographs
Plastics
RFID Tags (and other scanners)
Sanitary Clothing
Sanitary Wraps for food or other perishable items
Scratch-resistance coatings
Solar Panels
Switches
Termite treatments
Thermostats

Toasters
Utensils
Watches
Water pipes
Water purifiers
Weapons systems
Wiring

The Substitution Myth

There will always be the belief that if silver gets expensive enough, that other elements might be able to replace silver in some of the technologies or gadgets listed above. Obviously, if silver were to become more expensive than the platinum group metals (the cheapest of which is about 600 dollars an ounce), or gold (which currently resides around 1700 dollars an ounce) then maybe there is a point. But as of this writing, silver is still under 40 dollars an ounce! It will be a long time before silver becomes more expensive than the other precious metals. More realistically, there are metals like copper, which do have some of the properties of silver, and are much cheaper than silver. Some might say that you could replace the silver in your cell phone with copper, but there are huge drawbacks to copper in terms of its reliability. Your cell phone or computer likely would not be the same without silver, and under existing conditions, it is highly unlikely that copper would make any sort of decent substitute for silver.

So, in the final analysis, silver would have to explode to a very high value before other, cheaper (and less desirable) elements in the periodic table could replace it, if at all.

Bringing Back a Strategic Silver Stockpile?

For many years, the United States government maintained a stockpile of silver of several billion ounces (contrasted with today, where that number is probably less than 50 million, if even that). This stockpile not only existed for monetary purposes, but it also existed because the military might need silver in wartime. Since I have explained the many uses of silver in electronics, aircraft, and other weapon systems, it may make sense for the government to once again begin to stockpile the white metal. Another reason for the government to hoard silver may be in conjunction with other rare earth metals, such as those that are badly needed in the automobile industry.

In 2011, the President of American Elements, ironically named Michael Silver, talked about the need for a national rare earth stockpile. This was in response to the price of rare earth elements, such as Cerium or Lanthanum, increasing roughly 10 times in less than three years. (This may also be the kind of price action silver holders may experience in the coming months and years.) If the government had been committed to saving these kinds of metals, then possibly industry would not have to pay so much for them at present (or having to rely on China for them.)[27]

Any sort of official stockpile buildup in silver would represent an enormous change in the silver market. Few expect it, but few expected the crises of the last few years. The involvement of the "official sector" in the silver market is also related to the issue of "remonetization" of a metal that, although possessing every monetary characteristic of gold, has a collective value of only 5% that of gold on the world market.

The Remonetization of Silver

If we think about the silver price as firing on different engines, we have to acknowledge that only one engine-- retail or private investors (including hedge funds)-- propelled the price increase of the last decade. We have not seen a huge spike in industrial demand, and we certainly have not seen ANY demand from the "official" sector (meaning governments, central banks, or other large institutions.) But some wonder if this situation might not change someday.

As you should be well aware by now, over the last 150 years, the official, government sector has only been a negative for the silver price by selling billions and billions of ounces of silver coins and bars. But as related elsewhere, this trend has finally come to an end. Governments or other official entities no longer have much silver to dump on to the market. And, when you look closely, there are at least some people who are trying to bring back silver in one way or another. The fancy term for this is "remonetization." Whether or not governments officially hoard silver again, there are several movements and people out there who are working to increase people's understanding and use of silver as a monetary metal.

There are a growing number of people who see the use of silver (and gold) as means of savings and as a vehicle for honest economic transactions. Many groups advocate honest money, groups serving different constituencies, and representing different ideas. But there is a growing number of dissidents who believe that this monetary system, the monetary monopoly of central banking epitomized by the Federal Reserve, leaves a lot to be desired. There are several religious groups, for example, which believe that aspects of fiat money are frankly immoral. These groups run the gamut in terms of theological beliefs. For example, the Nation of Islam, as well as other branches of the Islamic faith, maintain that the decision to abandon a metallic backing to currency was an immoral act. Most will dislike the Anti-Semitic overtones of the writings of the Nation of Islam in particular, but it is hard to argue with the sentiment that individual people, and individual communities- whether we are talking about inner-city African-Americans, or rural white Americans- have a right to take back economic transactions away from the centralized banking state.[28]

In terms of private citizens influencing a government, one of the most prominent proponents of remonetizing silver has been Hugo Salinas Price. Born to a Mexican father and American mother, Salinas Price is widely respected by many hard money advocated on both sides of the US-Mexican border. In many ways, Price shares the concern of many in the US regarding how the US Federal Reserve and monetary authorities import inflation, or otherwise suppress interest rates. Of course as with many other Mexicans, Salinas Price has also seen unwise policies in Mexico City, which at least played a part in several currency devaluations over the last 30 years. Salinas Price has advocated the issuance of a silver dime as means of trying to familiarize the average Mexican with real money. The proposal put forth by Salinas Price would mandate that the silver coin always circulate at market value (or higher)- an important way of attempting to prevent Gresham's Law from taking over, since the coin would not be artificially capped by some sort of government or mint-mandated price. As a means of implementing his plan, Salinas Price heads the Mexican Civic Association Pro Silver, probably one of the more high-profile organizations around that is devoted to trying to bring back silver into at least part of the circulating medium of a country.[29]

American Efforts at Remonetization

In June 2011, the state of Utah became the first to exempt gold and silver from sales taxes, making it clear that people can purchase goods and services with the market value of gold and silver coins. This is important because it avoids encouraging people to simply hoard the money. But if market forces are allowed to exist, the likelihood of people hoarding the metal goes away- in fact, you might even see resurgence in the use of gold and silver money as a form of protest against unpopular banking practices. Republican State Representative Brad Galvez introduced the legislation to make gold and silver legal tender, and he hopes that other states and the US Congress will remove sales or capital gains taxes on gold and silver, as a means of encouraging trading with or saving in precious metals. While the law in Utah does not require merchants to accept gold and silver as payment for goods and services, the law is a clear shot across the bow of the Federal Reserve, and is one of several protests against fiat money.[30] At least one entrepreneur, Craig Franco is establishing the Utah Gold and Silver Depository as a means of allowing people to store gold and silver to back their debit cards in order to facilitate hard money transactions. Franco hopes that the IRS doesn't try to apply capital gains taxes to the gold and silver deposited with him, as this could be a sticking point not unlike the issue of sales taxes on gold and silver outlined above.

To me, it is not a coincidence that Utah led the way with the above efforts at remonetization. As many know, the Latter Day Saints, or Mormons, are quite strong in the state and the church has advocated that their members store up at least one years' worth of provisions, in addition to having some precious metal stored away. In fact, one of the more recent LDS Preparedness Guides (compiled by Christopher M. Parrett, chris@ldsavow.com) emphasized how silver coins are preferable to gold ones precisely because of their lesser value, and that members of the church may want to favor silver over gold in terms of storing cash. This guide also reinforced the notion that gold and silver are in fact money. (As an aside, I have to wonder how many Mormons actually take this guide to heart and buy anywhere from 50 to 1000 ounces of physical silver. Since there are likely 2 or 3 million Mormon households in the world, members of this one church could buy up anywhere from 10 to 50% of all known silver for investment.)

The Mormons believe in self-sufficiency overall, especially given the church's history of having to battle with the conventional world. Of most importance, the church emphasizes that someday wheat might even be more valuable than gold, since it is true that you can't eat gold or silver. The church's doctrine of storing up food and water, though, is not unrelated to a broad movement of getting off the grid, or of emphasizing local rights, and it is hard not to find similarity between the Utah gold/silver laws and the church's teachings on self-reliance. As of the summer of 2011, several other states, such as Virginia and Minnesota, are considering following in Utah's footsteps.[31]

Besides legal efforts to bring back gold and silver in everyday transactions, there are a number of possibilities for individuals in some part of the world to offer bank deposits that are backed by gold. To some extent, you already have this with online gold and silver accounts through bullionvault.com, or goldmoney.com, but these entities are not quite the same thing as a bank. One has to wonder if, in response to further money printing, currency shocks, or other financial mishaps, that someone may offer the option for people to save money, write checks, or otherwise transact with bank deposits fully backed by gold and silver.

The same could be said for mining companies choosing to hold more of their "cash" in the form of gold or silver, or for a corporation to hold more of their cash in gold or silver, since I have mentioned many times that cash is being treated like trash by the major central banks of the world.

Any or all of these developments would represent a major change in the "sponsorship" of silver, and would lead to a whole new price range for the white metal. The price of silver might not only move higher from average people trying to diversify their assets into metal; higher silver prices might come from the big players deciding that now is the time to make silver a part of their portfolios. And the amazing thing is, almost no one "big" has made this move.

The Coming Sponsors for Silver Investment

As stated more than once here, less than .5% of global financial wealth is held in silver. Silver is not yet thought of as mainstream by many. Perhaps it never will, and yet I know there are many institutional investors who may be getting desperate to generate returns. In early 2012, for example, it was revealed that the California Public Employee Pension Fund (CALPERS), made a measly 2011 return around 1% for the year. There was some commentary that, once again, pension funds like this are continuing to slip into the red in terms of their long term viability. This is due to two factors: one, states can only pitch in so much additional cash to help the funds meet their obligations, and two, investment returns have not done well these past several years for those in equities and (for the most part) in fixed income.

The inability of state governments to bail out pension funds is something that no asset manager can fix. Not so when it comes to ignoring raging bull markets in what has been termed the "fourth asset class": the precious metals. Nick Barisheff, of Bullion Management Group, has written how it is irresponsible for any asset manager not to take part in an entire asset class that has returned solid gains for nearly a decade. To those who say that pensions never "chase returns" (meaning following top performing investment groups) I would simply point out that pension funds in the 1950s invested less than 25% of their assets in equities– at the top of the internet bubble in 2000, however, that number had at least doubled.[32]

Very few public pensions that I am aware of have anything more than a couple of percent allocated to precious metals (the most famous example being the University of Texas.) Pension funds have not put much into gold and even less into silver. The same can be said of many other large investment pools, ranging from sovereign wealth funds, insurance companies, or mutual funds. The days of being able to dismiss the bull market in precious metals is coming to a close.

Peak Silver?

The idea of peak everything has made a comeback over the last ten years, and it may not be a coincidence that this discussion has paralleled the rising prices of many commodities since 2000. However, thinking about resource scarcity is nothing new. Many alive in the 1970s will remember the book *Limits to Growth*, which is still debated decades after its initial publication. Whether or not you agree with all aspects of that book's arguments, you would have to concede that ever-increasing growth rates lead to a point of resource scarcity. Also, to say that something has "peaked" does not mean that we are going to run out of a certain resource completely. In many cases it simply means that the growth rate in resource production cannot keep up with population or economic growth—but higher prices help preserve the resource by curtailing demand.

In terms of precious metals, there has been significant discussion of peak gold, at least judging from the frequency of the term on google (for what this is worth). The term "peak gold" registers a far higher count than "peak silver," and for good reason. Gold production- at least over the last decade- has failed to post the same 2-4% growth rates which occurred in the late 20th century. Silver mine production, on the other hand, has continued to grow at roughly the same rate (2-4%) as it did in the mid to late 20th century. So, at the most literal level, we will have to wait for peak silver. And it is not entirely clear that peak gold is a permanent phenomenon either, at least from a historical perspective. I say this because gold production has gone through periods of stagnation in the past, most recently from the 1930s through the 1950s. At that time, gold production stalled out around the 1000-1400 ton per year area, before resuming an upward move in the late 1950s.[33]

So even though we can't say if gold has peaked, we may be at peak production for quite some time- perhaps a very long time. For example, in the case of silver, estimates are that for most of the seventeenth and eighteenth centuries, silver production stagnated, and at many points actually declined.[34] Yes, eventually, silver production turned up again, but only after several generations of Europeans had to live with no growth in silver mining. Those people, during the course of their lives, experienced peak silver.

There are several reasons to be concerned about the possibility of some sort of peak or decline in silver production in the future. Here are just a few of the areas of concern, whether or not these factors will turn out to produce "peak" silver.

The Energy Return on Investment and Declining Silver Ore Grades

In 2009, Dr. A.M. Diederen produced an important presentation, "Metal Minerals Scarcity and the Elements of Hope" for The Oil Drum: Europe. He showed how at some point it is no longer profitable for any company to expend more energy to extract smaller and smaller amounts of mineral wealth. Additionally, if you believe in peak oil, it will be challenging to gain access to the requisite amount of oil to do everything from hauling rocks to pulverizing them in search of ever-smaller amounts of precious metal. Finally, Dr. Diederen relates how the percentage of certain minerals in rock has declined for many in-demand elements.[35] Similarly, Steve St. Angelo has compiled examples from the US and Australia revealing how silver ores as a percentage of geologic formations have declined by over 80% since the early 1900s. It is getting harder and harder to extract silver from the earth's crust, and one has to wonder when output reaches some sort of plateau.[36]

174

Lack of New Silver Mine Discoveries

According to Diederen, new mine deposit discoveries peaked at some point in the mid-1980s, with average annual discoveries, in his estimation, having declined over 60% since then. Diederen believes that large new discoveries of metals are unlikely.[37] This is a situation similar to oil, where the world has failed to find another Saudi Arabia in terms of reserves. The lack of new mine deposits leads people to question for how much longer silver mine production can increase if we are simply trying to extract more silver from the same locations that have produced silver, in some cases, for nearly 500 years (such as Mexico and Bolivia).

Silver production is held hostage to the prices of copper, zinc, lead and gold

Only about 20 or 30% of silver comes from primary silver production. In fact for many years the world's largest silver mining company has been BHP Billiton, which mainly mines alumina, other base metals, and oil and gas. In terms of percentages, roughly 25% of silver production comes from copper, and over 35%% from lead and zinc. The rest, roughly 10-15%, comes from gold (see both CPM Silver Yearbook and GFMS World Silver Survey). The fact that silver is held hostage to the prices of other metals influenced mine production in 2008. During this global recession, primary silver production rose much faster than silver produced as a byproduct, even as mine supply did increase over 2.5%.[38] At least in theory, if there were a huge surge in silver bullion purchases during a deflationary depression when base metal prices collapsed, it might be difficult to increase silver mine supply to meet demand.

Anemic Silver Reserve Growth Estimates

In the 1960s, the US Geological Survey only believed that there were about 5.5 billion ounces of silver reserves in the world. The price of silver at the time was roughly 1 dollar (1969). Of course, new reserves can be found and they were found, but the price needed to rise for that to happen. Silver reserves have grown: as of 2010, they stand at roughly 18 billion ounces, give or take. But it is important to note where the price of silver has gone since the late 1960s: it is up 30 times, to roughly 30 dollars an ounce, as of this writing. And of course 18 billion ounces of silver is only about 20 years' worth of silver mine production. One way to look at this relationship is that it took a 30 fold increase in the price of silver to yield a 3 fold increase in the amount of reserves. Over the last ten years, the reserve amount has only increased roughly 7% on an annualized basis, even as the price of silver has increased nearly 20% per year. So in order to get more reserves to increase the available silver from the ground, how much higher will silver go, if there is such a huge difference between the rate of increase in the silver price and the resulting increase in the reserve base?[39]

Among major commodities and metals (besides rare earth elements), silver has the least amount of mineable reserves relative to demand. In other words, if all else remained constant, we would run out of silver before other base metals, oil, or, even, gold. Of course, as shown above, the amount of reserves should increase (along with recycling) in the years ahead. But it is going to require a much higher price for this to occur.

176

Andean Countries: The Saudi Arabias of Silver

USGS reserve data for silver is subjective and relies on numerous sources (and guesses) from around the world. Still, I am amazed by how concentrated the reserve increases are by country (also note that reserves are different from the reserve base, an even more subjective number discontinued recently by the USGS). Between 2005 and 2010, only three countries accounted for nearly 70% of the 240,000 ton increase in global silver reserves. Those three countries were Peru, with an increase of 84,000 tons, Chile, which increased nearly 70,000 tons, and Bolivia, also nearly 18,000 ton increase. Of significance, Mexico- once a leader in silver production- saw zero increases in reserves from 2005 to 2010 (at 37,000 tons), and the United States, also a one-time leader in silver production, has actually seen its reserves decline from 31,000 tons in 1995 to 25,000 tons in 2010. So the growth in silver reserves, at least according to the USGS, is uneven and concentrated. The above information should also remind people how growth in finite resources can be held hostage to events or issues within very specific parts of the world. In the case of Peru- the world's leading silver producer in 2010- it was not that long ago that the "Shining Path" (a terrorist organization) seriously disrupted silver mining in that country. The same could be said about other developing countries who often resent outside mining interests. These countries could similarly disrupt successful mining projects for political purposes.[40]

So, as you can see, there are several reasons for concern regarding the possibility of peak silver someday.

The final reason for silver prices to possibly move much higher in the years to come is due to the possibility of people rallying around silver for political, philosophical, or religious reasons. In many ways, this reason is the most unpredictable; but it could also be the most powerful. In recent years, we have seen The Tea Party, Occupy Wall Street, or other acts of social protest in many parts of the world. I have already detailed how the internet has given more space for the honest money movement to grow and maintain followers. For many, owning silver is not about trying to make a quick buck but is instead a form of peaceful civil disobedience.

But I would not underestimate the power of people deciding to reform past actions, or otherwise change behavior out of a desire to stand on principle. I know that there are those moments in a person's life where the scales fall from their eyes, and they realize that they bought into (in this case quite literally) false hopes and false expectations of our modern way of life. A way of life predicated on all sorts of unsustainable beliefs and practices– whether we are talking about cheap oil, or endless consumption, or the idea that resources exist in infinite amounts that will never be made scarce by an exponentially-growing world population.

The history of money, wealth, and capital is messy and unfair. Once upon a time, the US emerged as the last man standing after World War II, and we had it on easy street (basically). But since the 1950s– notwithstanding some pockets of growth– the only way to go was down for this economy relative to the rest of the world. We live in a global economy, after all, and there are too many starving peasants who would love to compete for one dollar a day jobs, and there are too many other countries who don't care about environmental regulation or social welfare. These countries, it seems to me, are destined to eat at least a part of our lunch. You can subsidize industries, you can attempt to control or redistribute capital, you can even break up banks, but there are certain realities–like the birth, maturation and decline of great societies-- that are basically facts of history. In many ways, from my reading of history, I think it is just that simple.

Another fact of history is that modern finance, where capital is king, is a force of nature. Where once upon a time, people suffered from the seven lean years of famines or natural disasters, nowadays we suffer from contractions in credit and the collapse of asset bubbles. Unless you can devise some way to control people's minds and get them to borrow and invest in the exact right amounts, it seems to me that we are destined to ride the unpleasant waves of the business cycle. People pull back, they retrench, they become more conservative—ponzi schemes blow up. You can rail at the rich- and they deserve it- but it may not make much of a difference in your life if you confiscated all their property. Those evil rich people may have only been a part of the problem. Yes, too few of them went to jail for their crimes in the credit bubble, but how many average people were taking to the streets during the good years?

It may sound a bit corny, but I still think the most important path to any sort of social change has to start within people's minds and souls. To bring it back to protestors of any stripe, it may be that some of them are groping to deal with the scary nature of the truth that they are not part of the in-crowd, and that even if those in position of power or authority wanted to fix economies or institutions, they may be powerless to do so. It may be that the protesters are beginning a journey to build in their own lives, one by one, some sort of other, off-beat way of living. Maybe they will understand that there is just as much dignity in cleaning a toilet, or living on a farm in the middle of nowhere, as having a white collar job. Maybe they will realize that economies can suffer collapse without life ending. Maybe they are looking for other like-minded souls to find a meaning not given them in our present state.

Or, yes, maybe you have some professional agitators and bomb-throwers in the crowd. Maybe the crowd really does represent a fifth column of socialists trying to take over the world. Of course, we already have socialism for the rich, why not for the poor??

I am reminded of what Gerald Celente often says: "When people lose everything, they lose it." Just as I don't think jailing rich bastards would have helped things, I also don't blame members of the crowd if they decide to get unpleasant. Sometimes, all you can do is to make some sort of rude gesture at the injustice and rottenness of the world. As with any good existentialist hero, your life may not have any meaning until you begin to push back.

Pushing back can take many forms. So too can living a life consistent with principles. But the basis of morality in a society comes from the morality of exchange. What people receive for their currency, what they receive for their dollar, and is it fair? Many people feel that something is wrong with the exchange sanctioned by those who run our current world. Buying silver (along with other ways to opt out of our current economic order) is one small way to vote for a different set of economic or moral values.

The Ten Commandments from Planet Goldbug

What could be termed the moral imperative of investing in precious metals should not be underestimated, then, especially as part of the social movement wildcard that could draw many people to an asset like silver. However, it is worth pointing out how this kind of determined effort to take a stand for hard money has led some to famously quip that, as has been said, "gold (or silver) is not an investment, it's a religion."

This accusation goes back quite a long way, actually. The first negative use of the term goldbug likely started in the Election of 1896, as a way of criticizing the supporters of William McKinley who defended the gold standard. But the term first entered English via Edgar Allen Poe's short story, *The Gold-bug*, published in 1843. In the story, Poe relates the account of a man, Le Grand, who was bitten by a bug made of gold. The bite gives Le Grand supernatural power- clairvoyance really- to find the long-lost treasure of Captain Kidd (deposited somewhere along the southeast coast of the United States) in order to restore the Le Grand family fortune. At the end of the story, Poe has Le Grand relate to his friend that the power of the Goldbug was not what led to the treasure, but rather Le Grand's own reasoning powers, or ratiocination. But in keeping with Poe's usual portrayals of the mystical and terrific in his stories of ratiocination (meaning one's ability to reason in a superhuman manner) the reader is left wondering if it wasn't in fact the transcendent knowledge of the Goldbug which aided Le Grand after all. A large part of Poe's writing leaves room for intuition and magical insight, implying that these are as much a part of reason and intelligence as anything else. This

181

is an important point to keep in mind the next time someone derides gold and silver investing as a "religion."

Religion can mean many things—I simply take it to mean a belief in supernatural truths, or truths that are beyond this man-made world. I think that each day, more and more people are realizing some of these basic truths.

Here are some of what I would call the Ten Commandments of the gold (and silver) bugs:

1) Thou shalt not live beyond one's means.
2) Thou shall remember that if something sounds too good to be true, it is.
3) Thou shalt not rely solely on pushing paper wealth around for a living.
4) Thou shalt not place too much faith in politicians.
5) Thou shall honor the idea that resources cannot be conjured out of thin air.
6) Thou shall remember not to believe everything you hear, read, or even see.
7) Thou shall remember that what is given by the government can be taken away.
8) Thou shall take responsibility for your own financial wellbeing.
9) Thou shalt not steal from savers.
10) Thou shall remember how scientists, economists or other man made experts are not God.

These tenets are laid down only partially in jest. I really do think that as more people throw up their hands in frustration at the current financial system (and possibly at their role in aiding and abetting that system) people may also decide to reach for gold and silver. Not to make a killing, but to make a statement.

Only time will tell.

Chapter 6
Investing in the Silver Story (and knowing when to exit)

Bull markets are born amidst a skepticism where almost no one believes in the ability of an asset to ever make people money. This was the way much of the investing public felt about the stock market back in the mid or late 1970s. Who on earth would buy a stock? Equity prices had gone nowhere for nearly two decades. Pension funds owned far fewer of them in those years too. But then a great bull market in stocks began in earnest in the early 1980s, with not many people on board. It was only in the 1990s, over a decade after stocks entered a bull market, that the average person decided to buy into stocks. I think the same situation today applies to gold and silver.

Over the past several years, the market psychology surrounding silver and gold have been so negative that even many people who are concerned about inflation don't see the need to buy large amounts of precious metal. I encountered this when I spoke to a friend of my parents about what he was doing with his retirement money in 2005. This family friend had just sold a successful business but was concerned about the markets and wanted to make sure he preserved his capital. Makes sense enough. Like many people facing retirement, he was asking for advice from investment professionals and wanted a "safe" way to generate income.

But this family friend was also concerned about inflation, and he recognized that there were rumblings that all was not well with the US dollar. I was waiting for him to start talking about gold and silver, since both had recently broken out of ranges they had been stuck in for over 15 years. I was waiting, but he didn't talk about the need to buy gold and silver. Instead, his idea was to invest in Treasury Inflation Protected Securities. This was a strange idea in no small part because why would you expect the government to protect you from the very thing that the government is creating? This bears repeating—inflation is not some accident, it is a policy decision from governments that cannot grow their way out of debt burdens. So why would you trust the system to protect you from its own policy decision?

Slowly, though, I think that more and more investors and retirees will begin to catch on to how best to protect yourself against inflation (or attempts by central banks to create it) is with the ownership of real assets like gold and silver.

The issue of investor consciousness is an important one. As I wrote earlier, nothing lasts forever, things change, and you need to respect the wild swings that can be made by mass psychology. We may be on the cusp of a real change taking place, of an end to the kind of complacency that I wrote about above regarding gold and silver. For example, in 2011, the Gallup organization did a poll regarding which investments people think will outperform in the years ahead. The results were quite surprising: of the choices given to the respondents (stocks, real estate, CDs, or gold), gold received the plurality of votes as the best investment choice for the future.[1] And yet the numbers just don't add up. If 30-40% of people think precious metals like gold are the best place to be, then gold should be well over 10,000 dollars an ounce, since gold in no way comprises 30 or 40% of private assets. Many estimates put that number much close to 1-5%, as of 2011. I think many of these people are in the same boat I was six or seven years ago: watching a bull market, and wondering when to finally take the plunge to get in. For this reason, I believe the biggest move in the precious metals, believe it or not, still lies directly ahead of us.

Buying Physical Precious Metal: The Options

When it comes to buying bullion, I believe that you have to understand what you are trying to accomplish with your bullion (or coin) purchase. If you are trying to buy monetary insurance that you can use in the unfortunate event of a system breakdown (or if you think you might need to quickly access your wealth in order to leave the country), then you want to buy coins, minted by major world mints that can be easily stored. This would mean a combination of gold and silver, because gold is more portable, but silver will be easier for everyday transactions, especially in a barter situation. However, if you don't think that you might actually need your silver for everyday transactions (something I too think is unlikely), then silver bullion bars should be just fine.

One good website to use in order to compare dealers is goldshark.com. There you can shop around and see what the premiums might be for your coins. Understand that you will normally have to pay between 3-10% premiums for coins, sometimes higher. If you want to reduce your premium you need to buy larger amounts of coins or bullion bars. (For most people this would mean buying silver.)

In general, the best way to reduce your premium is to buy large bars of bullion. For example, 100 ounce or 1000 ounce silver bars have much lower premiums, generally, than smaller products. However, bullion bars are not necessarily great for everyday transactions, especially in larger amounts.

Another point to bear in mind is that in an industrial shortage situation, silver in bullion form is better to own, since they are already "market ready" unlike old coins, which are not bullion (normally 90% purity). However, oftentimes older coins (commonly called "junk silver") do not have the same premiums attached to government issued bullion coins.

The bottom line, I believe, is to diversify across different types of silver products without paying too large of a premium above the spot price (in my view, 10%).

If you choose to take delivery of your metal, there is the issue of storage. In this you need to use common sense. If you are really concerned about a currency collapse or civil unrest, then you will need the metal as close to you as possible. But you had better think creatively regarding where you will store your metal. On the other hand, if you are less freaked out about the world's future, a safe deposit box at a bank, or some other off-site insured depository will do just fine. The contents of safe deposit boxes are easier to insure. Just remember that there can be bank holidays and you might not be able to gain access to your metal for a certain period of time. The same can hold true of bullion repositories, by the way, since they may not be near your house or open all of the time.

Many other people don't want to deal with the hassle of having to personally store physical metal. These people use various options, ranging from online depositories to various exchange-traded funds that can be accessed through brokerage accounts. An example of online depositories include goldmoney.com; bullionvault.com; or silversaver.com.

Well known precious metals holding companies include the Central Fund of Canada (ticker symbol CEF) and the Sprott Physical Silver Trust (ticker symbol PHYS). These holding companies can be purchased through any major brokerage account and can be included in retirement plans. I would recommend dollar cost averaging into any of these investments, especially since premiums above the spot price do change. Another important caveat is that if you are holding your physical gold and silver through a brokerage account, you probably do not want to keep more than 500,000 dollars in any one account (which is the SIPC maximum), in the event of a brokerage bankruptcy.

In general, I believe you need to spread your physical precious metals around from the above groups. All of the above ways of owning metal have potential problems: storing metal at home can be dangerous and the insurance can be costly; safe deposit boxes or other off-site storage, on the other hand, can be limited in terms of access; and synthetic means of "owning" gold and silver are not the same thing as taking physical possession in the event of a real economic catastrophe. I also believe that you need to have some exposure to the mining stocks.

Why You Should Own Mining Stocks
(just remember they are not bullion)

Any person alive in the 1970s remembers the incredible bull market in mining stocks. Toward the end of that decade, there were many stocks that appreciated 10 or 20 TIMES in just a few years from 1978 to 1980. In conjunction with his boss, Doug Casey, Jeff Clark of caseyresearch has compiled a list of some of the returns made by gold and silver producers during that time period, and they are pretty impressive.[2] At least one of the better-known gold stock mutual funds from that period, the Van Eck International Gold Fund returned over 22% for the entire decade of the 1970s.[3] Going further back in time, to the Great Depression, there were three, large gold stocks that also made people money during a time when most stock investors lost their shirts. Homestake Mining, Alaska Juneau Gold Mining Company, and Dome Mines Limited, all had average returns of about 300% from 1929 to 1933, and this does not include dividends which were often north of 8%. The prices of Homestake and Alaska have been tracked by Mark Lundeen, with the help of Barron's Magazine, as part of the Barron's Gold Mining Index. Lundeen has shown that these two companies generated returns of over 100 TIMES for an investor who held them from the 1930s to 1980.[4] However, Lundeen and Barrons were unable to come up with more data regarding all of the other, smaller mining companies that existed during this period. These men aren't alone-- no major financial media publication or research institute has undertaken a serious study of the performance of all gold and silver mining stocks during the first part of last bull market in silver, from the 1930s through the 1960s. This, more than anything else, may be an indicator of how kooky and weird the larger investment world feels investing in gold and silver miners is. (Most major mining indexes, like the XAU or HUI were put together in the 1980s or 1990s.)

Still, anecdotal evidence shows that a diversified basket of large producers with some "juniors" in them easily produced returns in excess of 500 to 1000%, including dividends. Many South African miners actually paid out dividends at different points as high as 15% (if not higher.) Doug Casey, along with his associate Jeff Clark have published some of this data, and Doug included examples of major profits in the mining sector in his book, *Crisis Investing*, which was a national best-seller in the early 1980s.

What contributed to the mining stock mania of the late 1970s was the belief that earnings growth (coupled with the price of bullion) could only go one way: up. And not just up, but up big, as in annualized rates of north of 50%. If you know anything about Wall Street, you understand that speculators and institutional money will "pay up" for growth. You certainly saw this in the dot com bubble, where many stocks had price to earnings ratios in the 1000s- or worse yet did not even have price to earnings ratios because they had no earnings. But the belief was that everyone "had" to own these companies, which were hot and seemed to be a part of the best new thing to come along (the internet) since the invention of the wheel. (Understand that most companies don't have price to earnings ratios much higher than 10 or 15, and some would even call that expensive.)

But if the mood strikes Wall Street or other assorted speculators right, the same could happen to gold and silver miners as happened to the internet stocks of the 90s, or the mining shares of 1978-1980. Of course, this has yet to be the case, at least in the aggregate. Most of the major indexes which follow the precious metal miners have failed to keep up with the appreciation in gold and silver since 2008. Anecdotally of course, this also happened in the last bull market. A lot of the big gains were concentrated at certain times. It was either feast of famine with the mining stocks.

Some will also point out that the other reason the mining stocks have not performed as well has to do with the fact that there are so many more ways to gain exposure to gold and silver now through a brokerage account. In the 1970s, only the Central Fund of Canada existed (to my knowledge) as a kind of bullion equity that could be held in a brokerage account. Now there are several such funds.

But I am skeptical regarding this argument on five counts:

1) Mining stocks can pay dividends. They aren't back to 16%, but dividend payouts from mining stocks do appear to be growing. Recently, Newmont Mining essentially guaranteed increases in its dividend with the price of gold, as of the fall of 2011. As is often said about bullion to discredit it as an investment, bullion pays no income. Not so with mining stocks.

2) Mining companies can be takeover targets and you might benefit from the bidding war for assets. I should also add that with a mining stock you own gold or silver "in the ground," meaning a potential windfall if the next version of the California or Nevada gold or silver rush materializes.

3) It is important to remember that if you own gold or silver outright in the United States, you will likely face a higher tax upon sale than owning it in equity form (either through one of the trusts like the Central Fund, or by owning a mining stock.)

4) No one ever confiscated *all* mining stocks (though yes, some companies can be closed down by the government). In the bull market from 1930 to 1980, Americans could not legally own silver bullion until the mid-1960s, and gold bullion not until 1975. Along with rare coins and jewelry, another way to hedge yourself against inflation was with mining stocks. So mining stocks are an important way to diversify yourself against the political risk that your bullion will either be confiscated or taxed at a very high rate.

5) Finally, mining stocks do provide leverage to the gold or silver price, assuming that they can get their costs under control (or at least have their costs increase more slowly than the increase in the price of bullion.) For example, if a mine has a profit of 300 dollars and the price of gold moves from 1700 to 2000, it is possible that most of that 300 dollars goes to the bottom line (remember I said most, and remember this is a theoretical discussion). A 300 dollar increase in the bullion price was only about a 20 percent increase, but a 300 dollar increase to the bottom line of the mining company is a 100% increase! Hopefully you can see the difference. However, all of this is dependent upon Wall Street recognizing this story, and deciding that it wants to in fact pay up for this kind of earnings growth.

The mining stocks are just not well understood, and frankly, they suffer from the fact that leverage can work in two ways. In the example above, if bullion declines or if costs spiral out of control, then obviously you have a problem with your silver or gold producer. You also have political risk, or the risk of flooding, explosions, deaths, or environmental regulations- all of which could shudder the best of projects (this is why diversification counts.) It is true that gold and silver stocks are just that: stocks. They are not a substitute for bullion.

As of this writing, investors are risk-averse: this is one reason behind the interest in bullion as an investment. Most institutional investment houses simply do not believe that gold or silver prices are going to move higher. This is important, since institutional advisors or analysts often create a bullish or bearish mentality among big-money investors, and these advisors have consistently been conservative regarding the price of the metals. Obviously, if you are bearish on the price of the metals, then you don't want to own miners. But the group-think that dominates major investment houses is likely wrong, for all of the reasons I have laid out in this book. Just as there will likely be coming sponsors for bullion investment, so too will there be sponsors for the mining stocks, if the prices move higher in the way that I think they can.

Currently, the silver mining stocks (defined as companies who derive at least half their income from silver mining) only have a market cap of around 70 billion dollars. When coupled with the market capitalization of the gold miners, we get a number around 400 billion dollars, being generous. With the combined value of gold and silver bullion (mainly gold bullion, mind you) at nearly 8 trillion dollars, a 300 billion market cap for the miners is a VERY small number. Many older precious metals fans like to joke about "trying to put Niagara Falls through a garden hose" when describing how hard it will be for large amounts of money to find a home in these stocks without prices exploding higher. I don't care what anyone says about the ability of companies to issue paper so as to satiate investment demand: it did not happen with internet stocks in the late 1990s, and it likely will not happen with silver (and gold) stocks this time around.

Just as crisis consciousness is not the only driver for bullion investing, neither is risk aversion going to keep people away from the mining shares forever. Barring the end of the world, I think they will eventually get their day in the sun. And in that environment, it won't matter what the actual earnings are, what the actual feasibility of a project is, or what is going on politically. People will have gold and silver fever (like they had dot.com fever in the '90s). This irrational aspect of stock investing (speculating) may be unsettling to some, but I think it has a far larger grounding in reality than many realize.

In terms of silver companies, David Morgan has long advocated buying and holding Silver Wheaton, Franco Nevada, and Royal Gold as large, established mining stocks that can provide strong returns in the coming years.

For more on David Morgan's stock picks, see his paid service, silver-investor.com.

I also think that the three major mining ETFs aren't bad to include in a diversified mining stock portfolio: they are the GDX (large gold miners); GDXJ (smaller gold miners); SIL (exclusively silver miners).

Rare Coins and Jewelry as Possible Silver Investments

One of the more controversial aspects of gold and silver investing comes from complaints about "numismatics" or rare coins. It is true that there are various phone scams or other schemes to prey on people to get them to buy highly marked-up numismatics. I can't defend these practices, yet at the same time, I believe that if the average person were more comfortable with gold and silver investing, these schemes would get nowhere.

In general, bullion investing is the first thing anyone should do who wants to benefit from rising silver prices. Numismatics require another level of education, or sophistication. So I want to be clear that numismatics are potentially riskier than bullion.

However, in terms of rare coins, I also know that as with rare art, wine, or antiques, *rarity does count*. (I'll come back to this in a moment.)

As a gold investor, from 1933 all the way through to 1975, the only way to own physical gold was through jewelry or through old coins, or coins from small foreign mints that were allowed to produce these small, almost commemorative items. And as demand for gold in the 1950s moved the market away from the official 35 dollar price being maintained by Washington, all coins possessed strong premiums. Sometimes, these gold premiums would be as little as 10%, if market demand was not that strong, but by the 1960s, with the price of gold still fixed at 35 dollars an ounce, coin dealers reported average premiums near 25%-30% for one ounce gold coins such as St. Gaudens, Swiss Francs, and British Sovereigns.[5] In other words, it was impossible to pay much less than 38 dollars an ounce for gold, and you had to buy coins, if you were a retail investor.

In the case of silver, the premiums for American silver coins remained strong, even as bullion ownership was legalized in 1963. People will always feel comfortable knowing that they can use coins for transactions, and in some cases they trust government mints more than private mints.

There are two other very important points about the rare coin market. First, the rare coin market is not a futures market- it has limited to no leverage. In the case of the 1980s, this was important in the relative outperformance of many rare coins over gold and silver bullion. Rare coin investors are often different investors than those getting involved in the futures markets.

Second, the rare coin market is far, far smaller than the bullion market. If for some reason, a billionaire decides to begin collecting rare American coins, the coins aren't there. Many believe that the entire value of 19th and early 20th century American coins to be in the single billions of dollars, contrasted to trillions of dollars in bullion (mostly gold of course, not silver). So before you dismiss rare coin investing as mere "numismatics", you should keep an open mind. Bear in mind that people have made fortunes in this market, and that along with other forms of collectibles, they too may have their day in the sun, especially once inflation-consciousness sets in.

The leading source for information on American numismatics is pcgs.com, which is the website of the Professional Coin Grading Service. Numismaster.com provides a listing of rare coin dealers. Other companies I am familiar with include: Blanchard, H.S. Perlin and Company, John Hamrick, Stacks Bowers, and Teletrade. As always, do your own homework with this industry.

The Confiscation Issue

From any reading of history, you learn that government authorities have, in the past, tried to restrict people's access to gold and silver during times of crisis. This occurred most recently in the United States in the 1930s. But in this case, for example, I have to underscore the word "tried". Many people did not comply with government orders to hand over their gold, and the government did not try to confiscate all forms of gold and silver, only bullion. This is also an important point to remember when people talk about 90% "windfall profits" taxes in the event that the world goes back on a gold standard. It may prove to be quite difficult for the government or for any system to end private barter or exchange between parties in gold or silver at prevailing market rates. In addition, a 90% windfall profits tax on gold at 20,000 dollars an ounce (if you purchased at the current price of 1500 dollars) would likely still leave you with more than double your initial investment, which is not bad considering some of the lackluster returns of other investments recently.

Also bear in mind how earlier acts of confiscation came during a period when gold and silver were a larger part of the monetary system than they are today, and when you could formally devalue a currency by raising the price of gold (as occurred in the early 1930s.) Contrast this to the present, where we have floating currencies (some would say they simply sink at different rates), and where the metals are traded on highly leveraged futures exchanges. A far easier way to "confiscate" the wealth of people hoarding cash is to do exactly what the Federal Reserve and other central banks are already doing: don't pay savers any interest rates on their savings. If this is not confiscation, I would like to know what is.

What is worse, you have several calls being made to *charge* savers money if they decide to keep their money in "cash"—meaning bank deposit or savings accounts, or short term US Treasury debt, currently the most prestigious form of short term sovereign loans out there. Nominal negative interest rates (literally meaning you are charged for investing in cash or bonds) have briefly occurred among large banks since the 2008 crisis. These kinds of insanely low interest rates function as a type of confiscation, as an attempt being made by the authorities to stop the "hoarding" of cash by savers. Never mind that it isn't working, but it seems to me that the government has bigger fish to fry than those who invest in the relatively small gold and silver markets.

But there is another point here. If governments decided to try to restrict or confiscate privately held gold or silver, what would that say about the importance of these metals? Wouldn't it draw attention to the role these metals play as safe havens? Particularly for a central banker like

Ben Bernanke in the United States, who recently said gold was not money, if the authorities decided to make a stink out of people hoarding metal, I think it would undermine their efforts to ignore and marginalize the metals, particularly in terms of private transactions or barter. Outright confiscation would also be very costly to enforce, in my opinion, and likely would not be carried out globally. Moreover, as mentioned above, mining stocks have never (as a group) been confiscated, even as individual companies have seen their properties nationalized.

Silver Futures and Options

Given what I have written above regarding the paper silver market, I do not recommend that people put anything more than what they can afford to lose in leveraged, purely-paper silver. Understand that a futures contract is completely unbacked by metal unless you take delivery of the bullion—and be sure you take it off of the exchange vaults and into private vaults.

However, for the gamblers out there, you can trade silver through the Comex Exchange which generally gives leverage of roughly 15 to 1. There is also a FOREX silver market contract, which can be used against the dollar position (XAG/USD) to achieve leverage of 25 to 1.

It is possible to write put positions (bets against silver) as a way to hedge your physical position. This is a way of avoiding having to sell your metal if you are uncomfortable with the rapid ascent of the silver price (as happened in the spring of 2011 when silver jumped over 25% in a matter of weeks.)

As you might have guessed, I would encourage anyone who wants to gain exposure to silver to either buy it outright, or to buy into holding companies with verified stockpiles of silver. This is the best way to take advantage of the silver bull market.

A Note on Trading

There are those out there who will claim that they can make money trading. That may be well and good, and it certainly may be possible. However, I think gambling can be dangerous if it is not done in the spirit of the sort of realism I have described elsewhere. There are many who sell trading systems, many who believe that studying chart patterns or other technical indicators can enable one to jump in and out of a metal like silver, thus making even more money than having simply kept an original position. Some can succeed at this, just like there are expert poker players out there. But in reality, those who consistently succeed are few and far between. Just like going to Vegas, when you treat silver as another chip at a craps table, you might be surprised how easy it is to lose big in the short term, while others who had the patience to just hang on through the ups and downs make more in the long term.

And as I've mentioned more than once in this book, simply making money isn't everything, or, put differently, it oftentimes isn't enough to provide the kind of security many seek. We have all heard about people who make a million dollars a year, and yet manage to spend two million in that same year. So to repeat, just making money is not enough. You have to have the maturity and intelligence to live within your means, and to live a lifestyle that represents the outward expression of mental, emotional, and financial health. Too many people in my neck of the woods put their faith in consumerism, and I would bet that even as they appear to be wealthy, they are actually pretty poor. Without making light of those around the world truly suffering from poverty, I would bet that many suburban American, "middle class" people are far less happy than any number of people living in what used to be called "Third World" countries.

I believe the silver story is about how we all need to grow up. It is time for people to leave behind any number of myths or fantasies, including those of easy riches. What I have written here about the price of silver is not intended to be a get rich quick book. This book is about trying to wake people up, to try to help them become more financially-literate concerning where to put their hard-earned savings (or at least part of it.) This book is not about gambling.

I wrote earlier about how people often trade financial independence for perceived economic security. This often doesn't work out so well, or, put another way, there are downsides to having an economic system based on less and less self-reliance (even as many of us do not willingly want to go back to being farmers.) Making a fortune in the silver market may not mean that much if the health and well-being of yourself or those around you has been ruined by any number of financial or political mishaps. If you have lost political freedom, or if your society has been damaged by a collapsed economy or a dictatorship, wealth may only be of limited utility. The point here is not to scare people or obsess about future calamities—the point is to remind people of the need to keep perspective concerning what is really important in life, while also reminding people of the need to be prepared.

How High Could Silver Go?

And so there are several reasons not to be too focused on the fiat currency value of silver. Obviously, in a "toilet paper moment" for the US dollar, that number is not going to matter. Your physical silver is going to be an indispensable item for barter as the value of paper money collapses. But many of us even in the gold and silver community are not betting on the end of the world with our metal investments. So assuming that the dollar does continue to exist and that the world does not end, here are some realistic price targets—long term price targets, I might add-- for silver. These price targets are useful, I think, to remind people how far we are from a bubble in this market.

1)   The Case for 750 Dollar Silver

In the private market during the last silver bull, the price of silver was as low as 26 cents in 1932. It briefly hit a high just under 50 dollars in 1980.[6] I realize few people bought or traded silver at 26 cents, as there were all sorts of difficulties involved in doing so and trading in silver was suspended in the US from 1934 to 1963. But nonetheless, the market price of silver went up nearly 200 TIMES in 48 years. From the market bottom in silver just under 4 dollars ten years ago, this means that silver would need to reach roughly 750 to 800 dollars just to equal its last bull market. Remember that many observers feel the monetary and fiscal situation of our present world is far worse than during the last silver bull market, and that this silver bull could be EVEN BIGGER than the last one.

2) The Case for 2,000 Dollar Silver

According to the St. Louis Fed, the monetary base in 1980 was around 140 billion dollars.[7] Depending on what you believe the above ground amount of silver for investment was at the time (I think 3 billion ounces), this means that at the old price high in silver of 50 dollars, the value of the world's silver roughly equaled- if it did not exceed- the value of the U.S. monetary base. Today? The U.S. monetary base is over 2 trillion dollars, and yet there is about half as much silver in the world. What would the market price of all silver for investment need to be to equal the U.S. monetary base? Roughly 2,000 dollars an ounce, since today there is roughly 1.5 billion ounces of silver coin and bullion.

3) The Case for 3,000-4,000 Dollar Silver

Most readers understand that gold is still held as a reserve asset by governments and central banks, therefore making it the preferred precious metal in the world. Silver is no longer in this position, and is not sought after as an asset for purchase by central banks, sovereign wealth funds, and, as far as I know, is also not purchased by pension funds or endowments. But what if these kinds of official or quasi-official entities started to buy silver? Wouldn't this mean that silver was being revalued as a *truly* precious metal? One of the many paradoxes of the investing herd is that people do not like to buy things that are cheap, undervalued, and boring. They like buy things that are expensive, hot, and all the rage. I also believe that as silver goes higher and higher- and as it become more and more portable and easy to store in large amounts- you will continue to see ever more investor interest. Since there is only about a third as much silver as gold in coin and bullion form above ground, silver coins could possibly become more valuable than gold someday. Remember that once upon a time, the value of gold and silver at least approximated the relative above-ground abundance of the two metals. People have become so accustomed to thinking of silver as "the poor man's gold," that they have failed to notice that silver coins are rarer than gold coins. If I transported someone from the 17th century and told them just how rare silver was today but then explained to them that silver was less than 1/50 of the gold price, I'm sure they would grab every ounce of silver possible. You might want to think about doing the same thing if you have yet to buy any of this supposedly poor man's gold.

Some will also say that the above numbers of silver are not possible unless there is a collapse of the dollar. I suppose it depends upon what you mean by collapse. In the last silver bull, the dollar did lose over 70% of its value, but that collapse did not happen all at once. It essentially was a controlled, managed decline of the greenback. Currency debasement is the norm in the modern world after all and you might be surprised for how much longer debasement can go on without the world ending.

When Will The Precious Metals' Bull End?

What will things look like when this bull market in gold and silver finally comes to a close? You might be wondering. Of course, as you will see from the reasons given below, I don't think we are anywhere near an end to this precious metals' bull. I have history on my side in this regard, since the last bull market in silver went on for nearly 50 YEARS. And when you stop to consider the conditions that stopped the last bull market in silver, namely a Federal Reserve concerned about purging the system of inflation, an end to the precious metals bull is nowhere to be seen (the Federal Reserve as of 2012 is leaving interest rates at zero for the foreseeable future). At this rate, I predict it will take years (decades?) before you see a Federal Reserve that is interested in draining the monetary system of inflation. In other words, I think we are a long ways away from a top in the metals.

But here are some things to look for at the top of the precious metals bull market:

An end to the bull market in the metals means that we can all go back to the kind of leveraged debt games of the 1980s and 90s. It means that you will see another renaissance in the kind of debt-fueled consumption in the years before 2007. The end of the bull market in the metals means that the depression (yes thats what it is) will be over.

An end to the bull market in the metals will mean that there will be no more talk about the risks of rehypothecation (shell games in the financial system), about blackholes in the banking system, about counterparty risk. No longer will there be talk about systemic crisis, nor will there be any need for weekend summits in Europe to address sovereign debt levels, or people wondering about the breakup of currencies, or rumors of bankers or foreign leaders moving capital out of jurisdictions in danger of bank holidays or asset freezes. No longer will once powerful banks have to rely on accounting fraud (mark to make believe accounting) to see their stocks rise, and no longer will people be wondering about shorting said banks into oblivion because of their fundamental insolvency.

The bull market in gold and silver will end when countries like our own have finally dealt with the ticking time bombs of entitlement costs, of out of control spending. There will also cease to be complaints raised by our trading partners about the viability of the dollar as the world's reserve currency, no longer lectures from creditors about the profligacy of whole nations of insolvent debtors. Savers, like in 1980, will once again be compensated against inflation with decent interest rates (or positive interest rates.) There might be talk of how genuinely undervalued stocks are (for example, because they have dividends above 6 or 7%). There will no longer be a resurgence of interest on the internet in conspiracy theories, resurgent discussion of financial repression, or denunciations of "banksters" and enmity toward a financial aristocracy few complained about when times were better. We might once again see men like Alan Greenspan and Larry Summers on the cover of Time magazine.

The bull market in gold and silver will end when those of us who own these assets will no longer be ignored, smirked at, laughed at, or thought to be crazy for not realizing that there are so many other ways to preserve capital against systemic risk (like certain kinds of stocks or emerging market currencies, or short positions or puts.) Gold and silver will no longer be seen as backwater investments. Gold and silver mining shares will not be trashed with impunity by naked short sellers. The bull market in gold and silver will only end after the very banks and large institutions so often lamented for their short positions, go long. (Yes, it can happen).

As I mentioned earlier, in early 1980 the value of gold in the United States EXCEEDED the market capitalization of the US stock market by about 15%. This would currently put gold at over $15,000 an ounce. And I also already commented how in the case of silver, the value of the world's silver roughly equaled the US monetary base at that time. Today, this would yield a silver price of over $2,000 an ounce. At these prices, as in 1980, gold and silver may become systemically significant, meaning the authorities will have to revamp the world's currency and banking regime so as to stop capital from fleeing paper money and into hard assets (this is how I interpret Paul Volker's efforts in 1980-1 to dramatically increase interest rates—it was a way to save the paper money system.) Obviously, we have a long way to go price wise before the price targets mentioned above are met. Gold and silver are still—believe it or not—fairly well ignored by most investors.

One of the biggest risks, I think, for gold and silver holders going forward is getting off of this bull too soon. Perhaps ironically (or paradoxically) sometimes it takes a lot of courage to let your speculation ride to the top. Although I will admit that this is a good problem to have.

Will The World Return to a Gold Standard?

The main point that I have tried to make clear in this book is that several groups around the world are- at the margins- redefining the role of gold and silver in their portfolios. At the moment, such investing is simply as a hedge, however. This means that the average person who buys gold or silver maybe has 1 or 3 or 5 percent of their total wealth in precious metals, and many still have exactly ZERO exposure to the metals. Likewise most foreign governments have less than 5% of their currency reserves in gold. I have tried to stress that if individuals, governments, or banks decided to put 30 or 40 or 50% of their money into physical gold and silver, we would be talking about 30,000 or 40,000 dollar gold and silver similarly in the thousands of dollars.

So remember- I am not saying that people are betting everything on the precious metals. And you certainly don't need this to happen to increase the value of the two metals.

The hedging going on by, for example, the central bank of China, is not being done in anticipation of the complete collapse of the U.S. dollar. The Chinese themselves own too many Treasuries and hardly want the dollar to collapse (although many will point out that no one can predict or determine future currency accidents.) Rather, the Chinese are trying to diversify away from the Greenback and possibly create regional trade alliances that bypass the dollar. Ditto for India, Iran, Russia, or any number of other developing nations.

So, again, the name of the game so far has been diversification. It is not yet clear that any world power (let alone the United States) is planning to bring back any plan for convertibility, meaning that a certain percentage of bank deposits or cash can be freely exchanged into gold or silver. This does not mean that it can't happen, of course, nor does it mean that things won't deteriorate to a point where only by restoring convertibility will confidence be restored.

It is also no guarantee that our complex world economic system will collapse as quickly as some might claim. Yes, there are numerous problems, ranging from resource scarcity to political incompetence to currency debasement, but sometimes it is important to remember all of the apocalyptic, millennial movements of the past that failed to predict the end of the world.

Obviously, though, in a world that returns to barter, in a world where your electronic bank account or your brokerage account is not worth much- or in a world where the state simply confiscates electronic forms of wealth— black markets will likely thrive (or at least exist to keep people from starving.) Even in the darkest moments of totalitarian regimes, ranging from Maoist China, to Stalinist Russia, or Mugabe's Zimbabwe, people could still transact trade outside of official channels. In other words, the state cannot totally stamp out bartering. This links back to the point made earlier about silver and survivalism. When the- you- know- what hits the fan, people understand that the most important forms of wealth are portable and can fit in your hand (or are edible and can keep you alive.)

I hope you understand that while no one can predict the future, there are many reasons for silver to be much higher than today. Not all of them have to do with the apocalypse, and most of them, in my view, simply have to do with simple prudence and forethought.

You don't necessarily have to bet the ranch, as it were, on the metal. But I hope you have learned that silver cannot and should not be ignored by investors.

Acknowledgements

There are many individuals to thank who have assisted me in some way with the writing of this book. I have to begin by thanking my mom, Pauline Jordan, for her early encouragement to write something on the precious metals, which have been a quiet (now not so quiet) interest of mine for a long time. Elda Diaz Briseno helped encourage me, too, especially when it came to the Mexican angle of the silver story. Thanks also to Stephanie Doucette who came to the rescue with some last minute editing help. Then there are the editors of the many sites who have previously published my work, especially Cris Sheridan of financialsense.com, I.M. Vronsky of gold-eagle.com, and Kenny Parsons of silverbearcafe.com. There have been many experts, analysts, and friends who have given me important feedback on all or part of this book including: Bill Jacobsen, Alex Bueno-Edwards, Jeff Campbell, John Gonzalez, Peter Degraaff, Al Korelin, Mark Lundeen, Franklin Sanders, Steve St. Angelo, and Joel Perlin. Al Korelin was kind enough to interview me on his radio program as well as offer helpful feedback on some of my work. Jim Puplava of the PFS Group and Financial Sense Newshour shared some of his precious time for an interview with me regarding where he stood on the financial markets overall, for which I am very grateful. Special thanks go to Ted Butler and the staff of butlerresearch.com for not only answering numerous email

209

questions of mine, but for also sharing parts of Ted's book on silver, "Silver Profits in the New Century." Finally, I wish to thank David Morgan of silver-investor.com for his support, advice, and interest in this project, as well as for agreeing to write the foreword. I hope this book has done justice to his views, as well as to those of all of the other silver bulls out there.

Notes for the Introduction

[1] For a good overview of the nature of silver, see James U. Blanchard, *The Silver Bonanza: How To Profit from the Coming Bull Market in Silver* (New York, 1993), 21-29.
[2] For silver's monetary and cultural importance, see Jerome F. Smith, *Silver Profits in the Eighties* (New York, 1982), xvii-xix
[3] For data concerning the size of silver stockpiles, and of the silver market overall, consult: *The CPM Silver Yearbook*, CPM Group (New York, 2009), 3-27; and Silver Institute data for 2011 in "The Silver Investment Market- An Update," http://www.silverinstitute.org/site/wp-content/uploads/2011/12/silver-investment-market-update-nov-2011.pdf [accessed March 29, 2012]. Both institutes have slightly different numbers for categories like industrial demand or net investment purchases, but these differences are within about 20% of each other.
[4] On the reality of silver consumption (or destruction), see CPM Group, *Silver Yearbook*, 25.
[5] For a discussion of the palladium market in the late 1990s, see David Morgan, *Get the Skinny on Silver Investing* (Garden City, NY, 2009), 107-108.

Notes for Chapter 1

[1] There have been several books written on the modern, highly leveraged American real estate market and its damaging impact on the American economy. Two examples from different perspectives include: David Faber, *And Then the Roof Caved In: How Wall Street's Greed and Stupidity Brought Capitalism To Its Knees* (Hoboken, NJ, 2009); and Jerry Tuma, *From Boom to Bust And Beyond* (Lake Mary, FL, 2009), 41-85.

[2] A best-selling account of the dangers facing the US Dollar can be found in James Turk and John Rubino, *The Collapse of the Dollar and How to Profit from it* (New York, 2007).

3 Two accounts of the problem of derivatives and bank bailouts can be found in Dylan Ratigan, *Greedy bastards : how we can stop corporate communists, banksters, and other vampires from sucking America dry* (New York, 2012); and Barry Ritholz and Aaron Task *Bailout nation : how greed and easy money corrupted Wall Street and shook the world economy* (New York, 2009).

[4] Bank for International Settlements, "Deflation-Making Sure It Doesn't Happen Here," by Ben S. Bernanke, 2002, http://www.bis.org/review/r021126d.pdf [accessed March 30, 2012].

[5] For an account of the problems facing central bankers in the period from 1913 to 1933, see Nathan Lewis, *Gold: The Once and Future* Money (New York, 2007), 230-33, 237-38; Charles P. Kindleberger and Robert Aliber, *Manias, Panics, and Crashes: A History of Financial Crises*, 5th ed. (New York, 2005), 82-83; 138-139; 240-242 256-263.

[6] For John Williams' views on inflation reporting, see John Williams, "John Williams' Shadow Government Statistics," http://www.shadowstats.com/article/aa871 [accessed March 29, 2012]

[7] The above quotes can be found in Nathan Lewis, *Gold: The Once and Future Money*, 26, 73- 74, 88, 97-98, 106-107, 239, 295, 341.

[8] Lewis, *Gold*, 97.

Notes for Chapter 2

[1] Niall Ferguson, *The Ascent of Money: A Financial History of the World* (New York, 2008), 50-52.

[2] See Lewis, *Gold*, 153-166, 187-199 for a discussion of early American money and finance.

[3] Ron Paul, *The Case for Gold: A Minority Report of the U.S. Gold Commission*, second ed. (Auburn, Al, 2011), 30-31.

[4] Paul, *The Case for Gold*, 36-50.

[5] Paul, *The Case for Gold*, 75.

[6] Paul, *The Case for Gold*, 97-99.

[7] Paul, *The Case for Gold*, 126-132.

[8] Morgan, *Silver Investing*, 65-68.

[9] Shaw quote in Peter L. Bernstein, *The Power of Gold: The History of an Obsession* (New York, 2000), 369.

[10] Marc Faber CNCB interview, http://dealbreaker.com/2011/08/marc-faber-trust-no-one/#more-50606 [accessed March 29, 2012]

[11] The best account of the Weimar experience is Adam Ferguson, *When Money Dies: The Nightmare of Deficit Spending, Devaluation, and Hyperinflation in Weimar Germany* (New York, 1975).

[12] A good critique of the policies of former Federal Reserve Chairman Alan Greenspan is, William A. Fleckenstein and Frederick Sheehan, *Greenspan's Bubbles: The age of ignorance at the Federal Reserve* (New York, 2008).

[13] For information on 2011 gold investment statistics, see World Gold Council, https://www.gold.org/investment/statistics/investment_statistics/ [accessed March 29, 2012].
[14] For information on gold reserves, see World Gold Council, https://www.gold.org/government_affairs/gold_reserves/ [accessed March 30, 2012].
[15] For one of many stories on official Chinese views of gold and silver, see the Digital Times, http://digitaljournal.com/article/279166 [accessed March 29, 2012].

Notes for Chapter 3

[1] Silver Bear Café, *http://www.silverbearcafe.com/private/oneifbyland.html* [accessed March 29, 2012]
[2] Quote from Stan V. Henkels, *Andrew Jackson and the Bank of the United States* (private publisher, 1928), 7-8.
[3] Commitment of Traders Report for Silver, CFTC, http://www.cftc.gov/dea/futures/other_lf.htm [accessed, March 29, 2012]
[4] Data for short concentrations in orange juice or oats can be found at the CFTC, http://www.cftc.gov/dea/futures/ag_lf.htm [accessed March 29, 2012]. Inventory data for oil can be found at the EIA, "World Oil Balance," http://www.eia.gov/petroleum/data.cfm#summary [accessed March 29, 2012]; inventory data for orange juice comes from Bloomberg News, http://www.businessweek.com/news/2012-03-19/orange-juice-stocks-will-rise-to-535-000-tons-end-june [accessed March 28, 2012].
[5] For an interview concerning Chilton and the CFTC investigation, see FSN Newshour, http://www.financialsense.com/financial-sense-newshour/big-picture/2012/03/17/03/e-sprott-d-morgan-b-chilton/response-to-cftc-commissioner-silver-manipulation [accessed March 29, 2012]
[6] See Ed Steer's Gold and Silver Daily Report, http://www.caseyresearch.com/gsd/home [accessed March 29, 2012]; and for Doug Casey on silver, see Casey Research Reports, http://www.firstmajestic.com/i/pdf/2004-08-CR.pdf [accessed March 29, 2012].
[7] Jim Puplava, Financialsense.com, http://www.financialsense.com/contributors/jim-puplava/silver-undervalued-asset-looking-for-a-catalyst [accessed March 29, 2012]
[8] A good account of Sanders' views on silver and banking was done by Betsy Hansen, http://www.betsynhansen.com/2009/08/will-radically-different-banking-plans.html [accessed March 29, 2012]. Sanders own version is found

at http://the-
moneychanger.com/answers/the_most_dangerous_man_in_the_mid_south.

Notes for Chapter 4

[1] Jonathan Williams, ed. *Money: A History* (New York, 1997), 16-23.
[2] Williams, *Money*, 34-54, 11-113, 127-129.
[3] Williams, *Money*, 160-161.
[4] Smith, *Silver Profits in the '80s*, 43.
[5] Bernstein, *Power of Gold*, 193.
[6] Bernstein, *Power of Gold*, 196.
[7] Williams, *Money*, 20-26.
[8] Louise Buenger Robbert, "Monetary Flows- Venice 1150 to 1400," in John F. Richards, *Precious Metals in the later medieval and early modern worlds* (Durham, NC, 1983), 53.
[9] Harry A. Miskimin, "Money and Money Movements in France and England at the end of the Middle Ages," in Richards, *Precious Metals*, 83.
[10] A good discussion of the importance of silver as a monetary standard is Charles Savoie, http://www.silver-investor.com/charlessavoie/cs_3-29-05_monetarymadhouse.htm [accessed March 29, 2012].
[11] Philip D. Curtin, "Africa and the wider monetary world, 1250-1850," in Richards, *Precious Metals*, 260.
[12] David Hackett Fischer, *The Great Wave: Price Revolutions and the Rhythm of History* (New York, 1996), 336n.
[13] Timothy Green, *The Millennium in Silver: The Essential Guide to Prices, Production and Key Events* (London, 1999), 22.
[14] Williams, *Money*, 50-54.
[15] Halil Sahillioglu, "The role of international monetary and metal movements in Ottoman Monetary History, 1300-1750," in Richards, *Precious Metals*, 271-276.
[16] Williams, *Money*, 100-101.
[17] Lewis, *Gold*, 183-200.
[18] Smith, *The Millennium in Silver*, 10.
[19] Smith, *The Millennium in Silver*, 25.
[20] Smith, *Millennium in Silver*, 16.
[21] Smith, *Millennium in Silver*, 18.
[22] Bernstein, *Power of Gold*, 192-197.
[23] Roy W. Jastram, *Silver: The Restless Metal* (New York, 1981), 167-171.
[24] Jastram, *Silver*, 178-79.
[25] Jastram, *Silver*, 74-77.
[26] Bernstein, *Power of Gold*, 246-252, 256-257.
[27] A good account of the silverite issue can be found in Gretchen Ritter, *Goldbugs and Greenbacks: The Antimonopoly Tradition and the Politics of Finance in America, 1865-1896* (New York, 1997), 158-207.
[28] Murray N. Rothbard, *America's Great Depression* (Thousand Oaks, CA, 2008), 109-113, 132-38.
[29] Smith, *Silver Profits*, 169-186.

[30] Jastram, *Silver*, 95-103.

[31] Pierre Vilar, *History of Gold As Money*, 1450-1920, (London, 1984), 352.

[32] Jastram, *Silver*, 140-145.

[33] Jastram, *Silver*, 182-188.

[34] JP Ryan and Bureau of Mines, *Silver, Minerals Yearbook, Metals and Minerals*, (Washington, 1970), 1014.

[35] Jerry Markham, *The History of Commodity Futures Trading and Its Regulation* (New York, 1987), 179.

[36] Michael Maloney, *Guide to Investing in Gold and Silver: Everything You Need to Know to Profit From Precious Metals Now* (New York, 2008), 44-47.

[37] Quote from Harry Hurt, "Silverfinger,"originally published in Playboy Magazine, now cached at http://www.zerohedge.com/article/silverfinger-true-story-nelson-bunker-hunt, p.8 [accessed March 29, 2012].

[38] Timothy Green, *The New World of Gold* (New York, 1981), 160.

[39] Bernstein, *The Power of Gold*, 359.

[40] Two accounts of the Hunt brothers episode can be found in Hary Hurt III, *Texas Rich: The Hunt Dynasty* (New York, 1982), and Paul Sarnoff, *Trading in Silver: How To Make High Profits in the World Silver Market* (Chicago, 1988), pp.37-40.

[41] Regarding the quote and more about Buffett's purchase, see www.silvermonthly.com/analyzing-warren-buffetts-investment-in-silver, June 27, 2007 [accessed March 28, 2012].

[42] The Silver Institute, *World Silver Survey, 1950-1990* (Washington, D.C., 1990), 3.

[43] The Silver Institute, *World Silver Survey*, 29.

[44] Smith, *Millennium in Silver*, 25.

[45] Fischer, *Great Wave*, 171.

[46] Jastram, *Silver*, 185.

[47] CPM Group, *Silver Yearbook*, 25.

[48] Jastram, *Silver*, 197-199.

[49] CPM Group, *Silver Yearbook*, 150-51.

Notes for Chapter 5

[1] See this article by Carmen Reinhart, et. al http://www.imf.org/external/pubs/ft/fandd/2011/06/reinhart.htm [accessed April 2, 2012].

[2] Based on the commodity summaries at the usgs.gov site for both metals. For silver, see http://minerals.usgs.gov/minerals/pubs/commodity/silver/mcs-2012-silve.pdf; for gold, see http://minerals.usgs.gov/minerals/pubs/commodity/gold/mcs-2012-gold.pdf [accessed March 30, 2012]

[3] See USGS data for silver and gold for 2012 at usgs.gov, http://minerals.usgs.gov/minerals/pubs/commodity/gold/mcs-2012-gold.pdf; http://minerals.usgs.gov/minerals/pubs/commodity/silver/mcs-2012-silve.pdf [accessed March 30, 2012]

[4] CPM Group, *Silver Yearbook- 2009*, 25

[5] CPM Group, *Silver Yearbook*, 25.

[6] See data from the World Wealth Report, http://www.capgemini.com/services-and-solutions/by-industry/financial-services/solutions/wealth/worldwealthreport/ [accessed March 30, 2012]

[7] See data at http://www.wider.unu.edu/events/past-events/2006-events/en_GB/05-12-2006/ [accessed March 30, 2012]

[8] CPM Group, *Silver Yearbook-2009*, 11.

[9] See Silver Institute, http://www.silverinstitute.org/site/supply-demand/silver-supply/ [accessed March 30, 2012].

[10] Taken from CPM *Silver Yearbook*; and http://www.silverwheaton.com/Theme/SilverWheaton/files/docs_company%20fact%20sheet/World_Silver_Survey_2011_Summary_72011.pdf [accessed March 30, 2012].

[11] CPM Group, *Silver Yearbook-2009*, 8-11.

[12] One estimate of roughly 130 to 1 comes from the *Silver Yearbook*, 165.

[13] Bureau of Mines, Charles D. Hoyt, *Mineral Yearbook, 1969*, 1000.

[14] *World Silver Survey*, 1990, 52.

[15] *Silver Yearbook*, 165-169.

[16] *Silver Yearbook*, 165.

[17] Jerry Markham, *The History of Commodity Futures and Its Regulation* (New York, 1987), 6.

[18] Morgan, *Skinny on Silver Investing*, 99.

[19] Markham, *History of Commodity Futures*, 13.

[20] Markham, *History of Commodity Futures*, 26.

[21] Markham, *History of Commodity Futures*, 49.

[22] Blanchard, *Silver Bonanza*,

[23] Blanchard, *Silver Bonanza*, 22-23.

[24] See data from the Silver Institute, http://www.silverinstitute.org/site/silver-in-industry/ [accessed March 31, 2012].

[25] Herold, *Investing in Silver*, 104-105.

[26] David Morgan, "Silver In the Next Decade," [private paper, March 2010], accessed at http://www.silver-investor.com/members/pdf/SilverInTheNextDecade.pdf [March 31, 2012].

[27] See Industry Minerals report, http://www.simbolmaterials.com/documents/Industry_calls_for_US_critical_minerals_strategy_Industrial%20Minerals_March_2012.pdf [accessed March 31, 2012].

[28] One Islamic perspective on the value of gold and silver can be found at http://arshadmajid.hubpages.com/hub/Is-Paper-Money-Islamic [accessed March 31, 2012].

[29] For the proposals of Hugo Salinas Price, see plata.com.mx .

[30] One article on the Utah Gold Standard, is at the Huffington Post, http://www.huffingtonpost.com/2011/05/22/utah-gold-standard-silver_n_865333.html [accessed March 31, 2012].

[31] For Virginia, see zerohedge.com, http://www.zerohedge.com/article/virginia-creates-subcommittee-study-monetary-alternatives-case-terminal-fed-breakdown-consid [accessed March 31, 2012].

[32] For the views of Barisheff on portfolio allocation and the precious metals, see http://www.safehaven.com/article/21791/portfolio-diversification-myths-why-pension-funds-need-to-rethink-their-strategies [accessed March 31, 2012].

[33] See US Geological Survey, Gold Statistics, http://minerals.usgs.gov/ds/2005/140/ds140-gold.pdf [accessed March 31, 2012].

[34] Green, *The Millenium in Silver*, p.25.

[35] For the Diederen presentation, see the Oil Drum, http://www.theoildrum.com/node/5559 [accessed March 31, 2012].

[36] Steve St. Angelo, "Peak Silver and Peak Mining, http://news.silverseek.com/SilverSeek/1257346165.php [accessed March 31, 2012].

[37] See Diederen, Oil Drum, http://www.theoildrum.com/node/5559, slide 12 [accessed March 31, 2012].

[38] CPM Group, *Silver Yearbook 2009*, 31.

[39] USGS Silver Surveys from the 1960s can be accessed at http://digicoll.library.wisc.edu/cgi-bin/EcoNatRes/EcoNatRes-idx?type=header&id=EcoNatRes.MinYB1969v3&isize=text & the data from *Limits to Growth* regarding the 1970 reserve base for silver can be seen at http://seekingalpha.com/article/16152-limits-to-gold-and-silver-growth-supply-having-trouble-meeting-demand [accessed March 31, 2012] Data from 1996 to the present can be accessed at http://minerals.usgs.gov/minerals/pubs/commodity/silver/ [accessed March 31, 2012].

[40] Silver Reserve Data for the last several years can also be accessed at http://minerals.usgs.gov/minerals/pubs/commodity/silver/ [accessed March 31, 2012].

Notes for Chapter 6

[1] See the Gallup Organization, http://www.gallup.com/poll/149195/americans-choose-gold-best-long-term-investment.aspx [accessed April 11, 2012].

[2] See Jeff Clark, http://www.caseyresearch.com/cdd/50-gold-stocks-going-200 [accessed March 31, 2012].

[3] See Advisor Perspectives, http://www.advisorperspectives.com/newsletters11/pdfs/Investing_with_a_View_of_Significant_Inflation.pdf p.3 [March 31, 2012].

[4] See Mark Lundeen, http://www.gold-speculator.com/mark-lundeen/77176-barron-s-gold-mining-index-gold-silver-1920-dollar-terms-they-re-cheap.html [accessed March 31, 2012].

[5] See Bureau of Mines, JP Ryan, *Gold- 1963*, 1014.
[6] Jastram, *Silver- The Restless Metal*, 181.
[7] Federal Reserve Bank of St. Louis, http://research.stlouisfed.org/aggreg/newbase.html [accessed March 31, 2012].

36780284R00126

Made in the USA
Lexington, KY
06 November 2014